THE NEW GLADIATORS

MIXED MARTIAL ARTS REVEALED

THE NEW GLADIATORS

MIXED MARTIAL ARTS REVEALED

J. Alexander Poulton

OVER TIME BOOKS

The Publisher: OverTime Books is an imprint of Éditions de la Montagne Verte

Library and Archives Canada Cataloguing in Publication

Poulton, J. Alexander (Jay Alexander), 1977–
        The new gladiators : mixed martial arts revealed / J. Alexander Poulton.

Includes bibliographical references.
ISBN 978-1-897277-70-6

    1. Mixed martial arts. 2. Ultimate Fighting Championship.
I. Title.

GV1102.7.M59P68 2011   796.815   C2011-904980-5

Project Director: J. Alexander Poulton
Editor: Kathy van Denderen
Photo Credits: J. Alexander Poulton
Cover Image: George St-Pierre vs. Dan Hardy © Martin McNeil

We acknowledge the financial support of the Government of Canada through the Canada Book Fund (CBF) for our publishing activities.

Government of Québec—Tax Credit for book publishing—Administered by SODEC

 Canadian Heritage   Patrimoine canadien   SODEC Québec

PC: 5

Contents

Dedication

To my friend Richard Ho and the team at H2O Mixed Martial Arts Academy, and a special thanks to Olivier Aubin-Mercier for his help with the photography

Acknowledgments

This book would not have been possible without the knowledge and guidance of my good friend Richard Ho, owner of H2O Mixed Martial Arts Academy in Montreal. Over several lunches and phone calls, he let me pick his brain about the vast subject of mixed martial arts (MMA). Given the many branches of martial arts that came together to form the global phenomenon of MMA, Richard's knowledge of the sport and all its complexities aided me in getting down to the bare essentials. Our conversations were crucial to the formation of this book.

An unyielding army is destroyed.
An unbending tree breaks.
The hard must humble itself
or otherwise be humbled.
The soft will ultimately ascend.
Nothing under heaven is as
soft and yielding as water.
Yet for attacking the hard and strong,
nothing can compare to it.
The weak overcomes the strong.
The soft overcomes the hard.

–Lao Tzu, Chinese philosopher

Introduction

Fight Club was the beginning, now it's moved out of the basement; it's called Project Mayhem.

–Tyler Durden (Brad Pitt) from the movie *Fight Club*

Boxing is your father's sport.

–Dana White, UFC president

Weigh In

When mixed martial arts first burst onto the scene with the creation of the Ultimate Fighting Championship (UFC) in 1993, many people believed that it would not survive. Today, among all other major sports, the UFC and other leagues, federations and fighting networks make the wider discipline known as mixed martial arts the fastest growing sport in North America.

The UFC is now the highest grossing pay-per-view brand in the world, with earnings of over $465 million and with more than 9.3 million subscribers in 2010. At a recent event in Toronto, a record 55,000 fans turned in an estimated $10 million in revenue from the ticket sales alone. With numbers that good, MMA has forced many people to now take it seriously.

MMA is not just a North American phenomenon, either; the sport is truly global in its reach. The roots of the sport can be traced back through several different branches in several different countries that have a tradition of martial arts. Muay thai in Thailand, judo in Japan, wrestling in the United States and kung fu in China are all disciplines that have added their piece of the puzzle to the creation of MMA-style fighting, some more than others. For centuries, these disciplines never met each other on the battlefield, but as the world got smaller and karate met muay thai, and judo met Greco-Roman wrestling, the question of which fighting style was the best and the most effective naturally surfaced. The desire to answer that question eventually led to the creation of companies like the UFC, whose goal was to provide the place where fighters of all disciplines could test their skills.

However, not everyone was warm to the idea of two men beating on each other with bare fists.

Although no-holds-barred fighting flourished in countries like Brazil, and with some regulations put in place in Japan, when MMA was introduced into the North American market, it was met with both interest and disgust. The first UFC event marketed as "no rules fighting" did its job in attracting the 18- to 35-year-old male demographic, but almost everyone else reacted with contempt at the sight of men getting kicked or bashed in the face for entertainment. It was hard to blame viewers for their reactions; for the first few years, the UFC was marketed like a sideshow, with fighters like the giant sumo wrestler Emmanuel Yarborough put up against men half their size. The discipline of MMA got lost in the hype of trying to sell a product. But behind all the theatrics hid an honest sport that needed proper guidance to find its way into the regular lexicon of the sporting world.

While a fierce battle raged in the United States and Canada to ban ultimate fighting in the mid to late 1990s, the Japanese were open to the sport and welcomed the world's exiled fighters into their organizations, such as Pride, Rings and Pancrase. These outfits had instituted sets of rules and regulations that allowed for open and fair competitions and gave the sport a structure that it so desperately lacked in the UFC. With interested audiences and tons of money calling them, most North American fighters flew to Japan to compete and make a name for themselves while the U.S. and Canadian governments worked on their issues with the sport.

Fighters such as Ken Shamrock, Royce Gracie, Gary Goodridge, Dan Severn and many more who made a few thousand dollars fighting for the UFC in front of a handful of fans could now make hundreds of thousands of dollars in Japan, fighting before thousands of fans. Ken Shamrock became a bonafide superstar with a fan club, and he even appeared in Japanese comic books. The Japanese, who had a long tradition of wrestling and martial arts competitions, were not squeamish about two fighters beating on each other until one of them was knocked out or submitted. After all, it was a Japanese student of judo who had traveled to Brazil and schooled the Gracie family in a new style of fighting, one that the Gracies developed and eventually exported to the United States, leading to the creation of the UFC.

But not all was golden in the land of the rising sun. Although MMA was accepted, not all of the promotions delivered the kind of sport people were hoping to see. Pancrase, while initially successful, was deemed too timid by many fight fans because of the organization's restrictive rules and requirements that fighters wear leg and elbow pads. There was also the sense that several of the fights had been staged to make some fighters look better. As a result, Pancrase did not last long. Fans demanded reality, and the Rings network tried to provide that, but it was dogged by internal issues and the need to prop up their Japanese stars with staged fights. Japanese fight fans in 1993 had seen the example of the UFC and wanted to see the same brutal reality.

The Pride organization provided what the fans wanted. While North America was asleep to the possibilities of ultimate fighting, the rest of the world turned its eyes on Japan, where some of the most exciting fighters on the globe gathered. Fans were introduced to fighters like Kazushi Sakuraba of Japan, famous for his destruction of the once indestructible Gracie clan, from patriarchs Helio and Carlos to Rickson, and Fedor Emelianenko, the quiet Russian fighter with fists of steel.

With all eyes on the Japan fight networks, the UFC was near collapse, and all other North American MMA leagues were in jeopardy of being pushed out by the political will of a small but powerful minority. When all hope seemed lost for a future in North America, a small, dedicated group of people committed to the sport continued to advocate for acceptance, and though the sport was eventually accepted, it was still on the fringe. What MMA needed was money. That's when the Fertitta brothers, Las Vegas casino moguls, stepped in and purchased the UFC from its original owners.

As the 21st century dawned, ultimate fighting went from being an outlawed event to a respected sport with legions of fans. It was about athletes who had trained their whole lives, just like athletes in any other sport. Most people had discussed the sport in terms of its brutality, but now, the talk was of technique, skill and intelligence. Fighters such as Royce Gracie and Ken Shamrock were the essential reasons for the sport's initial success in gaining a foothold in the sports market at a time when the majority of the public viewed the UFC as more of a sideshow. Other fighters such as Matt Hughes, B.J. Penn, Georges St-Pierre, Randy Couture and many others also began to change public opinion. They showed the world that although the sport might appear brutal on the outside, the fighters put a lot of thought and technique behind everything they did. Gone were the days of the bar brawler, and in entered the focused athlete.

Why Fight?

The painful warrior famoused for fight,
After a thousand victories once foil'd,
Is from the book of honour razed quite,
And all the rest forgot for which he toil'd

—William Shakespeare

Everybody is fighting something.

—Renzo Gracie

Why fight? This is a question many people ask when seeing an MMA tournament for the first time. Why would a grown man put himself in an arena with an opponent whose goal is to bash his face in? On the surface, the competitors seem to have some masochistic need for pain, a primal desire deep within to take on a challenger to prove that they are the strongest.

We tend to look at athletes as being merely one-dimensional figures who in post-match interviews say nothing more than one-line clichés that every fan can almost mouth along with them: "It was tough out there, but we gave it 100 percent," or, "I just go out and do what I learned in training."

But MMA fighting occupies the dark fringes of the sporting world where beyond the simple victory or defeat lies something deeper. Hidden under the surface of those who give every part of themselves over to this brutal pursuit is the hardened will of a true warrior.

Imagine what it takes to step inside the ring: the years devoted to a single purpose; the hours spent at the gym; the dedication to proper nutrition; and the time spent away from other areas of their lives to achieve peak form. But the physical preparation is only a small part of a fighter's training. The will to fight and to put yourself in harm's way requires more than a muscular body; it takes the heart and mind of a warrior. It is a fighter's skill set that enables him to beat his opponent who has also spent equal amounts of time in the gym training. While many martial arts focus on perfecting the body, they also spend as much time working on the mental preparedness of the fighter.

These aspects of MMA fighting are often over-looked by the sport's detractors. Although on one level it is seen as a primal battle of survival—and the athletes pay a savage price for the bashing of flesh and bone—a mental chess match between opponents begins even before the fight starts.

Not many people can imagine the sheer will that it takes for fighters to step inside the ring, octagon or whatever venue that gives them no way out, except through the power of their fists and strength of their jaw. However, each and every fighter is not much different from the aver-age man on the street. Everyone takes on differ-ent challenges in their lives, succeeding or failing as the fighter does in the ring. It's just that MMA fighters take the rush of life to a higher level of intensity.

It is a level of courage most people only wish they could carry into their daily lives. But as well as having the courage to enter the cage and con-front another human being in battle without running away screaming, MMA fighters all have another trait in common: toughness. You need to be tough if you want to survive. No matter how good a grappler a fighter is, no matter how skilled his boxing, he has to think his opponent is just as good. It is the intangible that makes a great fighter. He has to enter the ring with purpose, courage and a determination that could out-match even his strongest foes. Physical as well as mental fortitude is required. Mental strength allows the fighter to get through the last minutes of a bout and to find another reserve of energy when there seemed to be none to push through the fight toward victory.

One of my favorite fighters, Fedor Eme-lianenko, is the perfect example of a man with mental and physical strength. His opponents have been the same size and weight as him and had the same amount of muscle and same amount of training, but Fedor could reach another stage when the fight seemed completely lost to him. In many of his fights, he appeared on the verge of being knocked out or close to sub-mitting, or in one bout, to have suffered a broken neck, but he often managed to come back in the most intense and entertaining ways. His level of toughness, both physical and mental, allowed him to prevail over the strongest opponents and get out of the most hopeless of situations.

Without a certain amount of toughness, fear would stop you from even entering the ring. Ulti-mate fighting is a hard-hitting sport, and fighters must overcome fear to succeed. This is without a doubt not an easy task to do. It is human nature to feel fear and to want to escape from all forms of violence. Writer Barbara Ehrenreich, in her book *Blood Rites,* tried to understand this natural human aversion to violence and how it might have led to our obsession with violence. She says that *Homo sapiens,* for most of our evolutionary history, were prey to larger, stronger and more agile animals. Our natural inclination was to flee from threats and to form groups for survival. As Ehrenreich states:

>...*our peculiar and ambivalent relationship to violence is rooted in a primordial experience that we have managed, as a species, to almost entirely repress. And this is the experience, not of hunting, but of being preyed on by animals that were initially far more skillful hunters than ourselves.*

It is her theory that our rise to the top as an "apex predator" was more of a social construct than an evolutionary one. Our wiring is still that of the terrified ape on the savannah running away from a predator. Ehrenreich argues that in overcoming the instinct to flee, we achieve a euphoric release from the fear we feel, thus becoming the apex predator. It is this euphoria that has led to humanity's glorification of war. We see this in the hunter who raises his arms in victory over his kill or in the soldier triumphant on the battlefield. This aspect of humanity can be seen in our more "refined" culture through our sports, and it is best exemplified in the world of fighting.

If any fighter were to tell you there was no fear in his heart before stepping into the ring, he probably would be lying. Fear of what might occur must weigh heavily as he steps into the ring, but it is the possibility of overcoming his opponent that drives the fighter on. The primordial victory over a predator makes us cheer from the stands or from our couches. We all want to be the apex predator, and so we root for the athlete we feel most close to and who gives us that euphoric triumph. For many of us, our hearts beat just as fast and our minds race as much as our favorite fighter facing a larger opponent. These fighters are human like us, but they choose to enter a cage or a ring with another human being and test the limits of what they are made of.

But the quest to be the toughest and most feared in the world is an empty one. There will always be a better opponent, someone bigger and someone stronger. Fighters who take that journey to prove they are the toughest will no doubt find nothing but emptiness, heartache and disappointment. A fighter might end up the best in a certain class or a certain country, but someone is always waiting in the wings to take that status away from him. For the true practitioner of any sport or martial art, it's about being the best you can and achieving that level when it counts the most. The greatest figures in all of sports achieved their highest levels of success at the right moments in their careers. It is the same with the fighters in MMA.

The real fighters, the ones who have experienced all sorts of adversity, truly understand why they fight. They leave their egos on the sidelines and test their skills to see if they are better than the next guy. It's not about who is the bigger man. "It's a form of enlightenment; lack of fear leads to nobility of character. Not all fighters develop this, but a surprising number do; the really good ones seem to," writes Sam Sheridan in his book *A Fighter's Heart*. The fighters undergo a type of spiritual transformation during competition, in pursuit of the perfect challenge of will, courage, fear and toughness. That is why they fight, and that is why we enjoy watching them fight.

Long before MMA achieved its incredible level of public acceptance that it has today, no-holds-barred fighting took place in dark alleyways at the back of shady bars or in the dank cathedral-like spaces of abandoned factories. Here existed an underworld of fighters waging blood and body for nothing more than the thrill and a nice payout. Despite the popularity of boxing and wrestling in North America, no-holds-barred fighting had no structure and no system, remaining a counter-culture phenomenon for the amusement of gangsters.

Internationally, underground tournament-style fighting has been around for centuries as practitioners of the martial arts would occasionally meet in an organized battle to test their skills against others. History and novels alike are filled with examples of ancient tournaments organized by shadow societies pitting highly skilled warriors against one another in deadly combat. But these were fringe events obscured by veils of secrecy. For the longest time, the idea of legitimizing this brand of fighting remained impossible to foresee, and it stayed in the shadows where most people felt it belonged.

However, to a new generation raised on the Rocky films, kung fu movies and video games, the idea of taking this ultimate style of fighting and legitimizing it began to take shape. More specifically, movies like Bruce Lee's *Game of Death,* and *Bloodsport,* starring Jean-Claude Van Damme, had tried to answer the question of which martial art was the best. The characters in both those movies entered into a competition against opponents skilled in martial arts from around the globe. The world eventually tried to answer the question with the formation of UFC and other fighting leagues, but these organizations did not spring up overnight. Mixed martial arts had a beginning.

The Evolution of Fighting

We learn to employ the principle of maximum efficiency even when we could easily overpower an opponent. Indeed, it is much more impressive to beat an opponent with proper technique than with brute force.

–Jigoro Kano

Our lives are repetitious shams—every single day a simulacrum of the previous day. So for Man, he is out to pepper his daily activities with different things—he's fighting against boredom.

–Matthew Lotti

Violence is a part of our species. From the most ancient cultures to the 21st century, men (mostly) have engaged in all forms of hand-to-hand combat imaginable. Its importance can be seen in the variety of fighting styles human beings have created throughout history. Using our creative powers, we have turned fighting into more than a mere tool for survival—humanity has turned fighting into an art form as well as a sport.

One of the earliest types of combat sports ever recorded can be traced back to the ancient tribes of the Tigris and Euphrates in what is now modern-day Iraq. Artifacts have been found that show the people practiced a type of boxing for entertainment, pitting two men against one another in a barefisted fight until only one of them was left standing. The ancient Greeks later developed a form of organized fighting called Pankration (literally, "to show power") in which two opponents fought in a no-holds-barred battle until one fighter submitted. In ancient Asia, the Chinese and Japanese further developed complex fighting methods of their own such as gung-fu and karate, which added the element of spirituality to fighting. Weapons were introduced, but at its core, for true practitioners of the martial arts, the real test of your skill remained in the hand-to-hand combat.

While the martial arts flourished in many societies in the East, in the Western world, hand-to-hand combat remained in its purest form in boxing. Although bare-knuckle fighting was popular through the ages in Eastern Europe, in the rest of the continent it remained a fringe activity practiced by young men under the heavy influence of alcohol, hoping to prove their masculinity. It was in 17th- and 18th-century England where the natural human inclination to fight was turned into a standardized system of organizationally and aesthetically coherent moves that gave each fighter an equal chance at victory.

At first, these bouts were nothing more than organized barefisted battles between men, but soon, gentlemanly rules—such as banning hits below the belt, head butts and kicking—were introduced. The rounds lasted a set time with breaks in between. Eventually, protective padding on the fists was used, and the modern form of boxing was born.

It was this format that made its way over to North America and became the most popular combat sport on the continent. Practitioners such as Jack Johnson, Rocky Marciano, Muhammad Ali and Mike Tyson were long considered some of the toughest men in the world. Their large hulking frames and powerful punches became the stuff of legend in the hands of writers such as Norman Mailer. For example, take Mailer's

poetic description of the fighter in his 1975 book
The Fight:

> *Not many psychotics could endure the disci-*
> *plines of professional boxing. Still, a heavy-*
> *weight champion must live in a world where*
> *the proportions are gone. He is conceivably the*
> *most frightening unarmed killer alive. With his*
> *hands he could slay fifty men before he would*
> *become too tired to kill any more. Or is the*
> *number closer to a hundred?... Prizefighters do*
> *not, of course, train to kill people at large. To*
> *the contrary, prizefighting offers a profession*
> *to men who might otherwise commit murder in*
> *the street.*

As travel became accessible, more people were
exposed to the different forms of martial arts
throughout the world, and a question became
obvious: which style of fighting was the best?

New forms of martial arts began to be seen in
North America for the first time in the 1800s,
and when compared to these established types of
Eastern fighting disciplines, boxing did not seem
to measure up as one of the best. The public
began to become aware of disciplines such as
muay thai from Thailand, the Japanese art of
judo, the myriad styles of Chinese kung fu and
the uniquely Brazilian fighting style known as
capoeira, among others. Practitioners of these

martial arts often traveled throughout the Western world promoting their fighting style as superior, and they took on all challengers.

Growing out of this demand from the public to see fights pitting different styles against each other, several organizations developed around the world separately from one another. In Japan, Brazil, the United States, Russia, Mexico and Thailand, the various branches of martial arts all began moving toward each other. At one time, martial arts practitioners simply stuck to one discipline and became masters of that fighting style.

In 1945, it would have been unusual to find a wrestler trained in boxing or a kung fu master skilled in muay thai, but as athletes were exposed to the various disciplines and incorporated some of the techniques into their own practice, the original style was altered. Such a cultural exchange is clearly demonstrated in the history of judo and how it borrowed techniques from Western wrestling. All these branches of martial arts eventually began to merge, leading to the creation of one of the most exciting sports on the planet.

For most fans of mixed martial arts, the sport seemed to come out of nowhere. But, in fact, the sport has a history that dates back many years through some surprising avenues.

The Rise of the Judoka

Developed in Japan likely around the 14th century, jujutsu (or "jujitsu," but more commonly known as "jiujitsu") is a method of close combat in which the fighter does not use a weapon. Loosely translated to mean "gentle technique or art," jiujitsu was developed as a way to manipulate an opponent's own force against himself rather than confronting brute force with brute force.

Before the rise of jiujitsu, the martial arts was dominated by the samurai tradition of swords and weaponry. However, swords and arrows aren't always effective in battle at close range, and out on the battlefield, a warrior was often forced to confront an enemy up close to try to defeat him using a dagger or, more often that not, his bare hands. Jiujitsu evolved out of this need for a system of close combat, focusing on techniques that included striking, throwing, grappling and the use of light weaponry such as daggers and chains.

Over time, many types of jiujitsu were created in Japan, with each method focusing on grappling techniques or using weapons. Jiujitsu schools sprang up across Japan, resulting in hundreds of different styles. By the 17th century, Japan had over 2000 jiujitsu schools dedicated to spreading the martial art. But by the 19th century, Japan had opened up to the world, and the culture of the samurai began to fade. With the death of the samurai, the jiujitsu schools' importance in the new world seemed archaic and pointless. Schools that normally were selective of the students they took in now had to accept all newcomers in an effort to survive. As a result, the students who enrolled in the schools tended to be common thugs and young gang members.

For true believers in the martial arts, the jiujitsu schools had lost their way. From their beginnings, these schools were more than simple places where students would learn deadly fighting techniques. The martial arts focused as much on philosophy as they did on fighting, mixing the ancient Japanese beliefs of Buddhism, Taoism, Shinto and Confucianism. Out of this system of beliefs came various states of mind that jiujitsu practitioners believed were essential to victory in battle.

First, the warrior had to cultivate a sense of awareness of the world and his place within it. This simply meant that the fighter had to be ready for anything at any time, because in the real world, danger can arise at a moment's notice. The second most important tenet of jiujitsu and of most martial arts is that the student must act without conscious thought. This sounds counter-intuitive to anyone who has not practiced a martial art, but it is one of the most essential mental techniques. Once a fighter is able to detach his mind from the movements of his body, only then can he react instantaneously and become much more effective in battle. The third principle is that of the "immovable mind," an unflappable mental state that allows the fighter to control his thoughts and attitude no matter what lies before him.

However, these principles of jiujitsu were pushed aside in the new Japan that had opened up to Western ideas of science, progress and technology. As a result, the serious student of martial arts who wanted to train in both the mental and physical forms of jiujitsu was left with few options in Japan during the 19th century. It was in this climate of social, political and cultural change that Jigoro Kano grew up.

A small, frail man even into his 20s, Jigoro Kano was often picked on by bigger kids at his school. Frustrated at the constant bullying, he decided to take up jiujitsu to defend himself. At first, this proved difficult for the diminutive Kano, as no school would take on a student of his stature, thinking him feeble. But he eventually found a school and began his training. Throwing himself into mastery of the art, Kano distinguished himself as one of the top students by the time he was 21.

However, Kano was not a man to limit himself to what he was taught, and throughout his training he constantly tried to improve upon the martial art. What he began to notice across Japan was that his beloved jiujitsu had become overrun with students eager to fight and who wanted to use those techniques out on the street. Jiujitsu had become a mixed bag of fighting tricks and was not the mindful philosophical discipline that the samurai had practiced long ago.

Jiujitsu had lost its way, and Kano felt it was his responsibility to bring a new respect back to the martial art by focusing on proper techniques and mental readiness. At the various schools he was attending, Kano was never completely satisfied with the way he was being instructed. He spent time outside of the jiujitsu schools and started to perfect techniques that he felt were more efficient in achieving the goal of making an opponent submit. He borrowed ideas from Western wrestling such as the firefighter carry or shoulder wheel, in which an opponent is thrown to the ground over the shoulder.

Kano had in mind a complete reformation of jiujitsu, with techniques based upon sound principles of body movement, action and reaction, and focusing on the development of a student's body, mind and proper character. After earning his university degree, Kano took on nine students of his own and began to implement his changes to the old form of jiujitsu. His new school of thought was originally known simply as Kano-jujutsu, but to distinguish his new style from the rest, he named his school Kodokan Judo to reflect his new theory of martial arts.

The word "judo" shares the same root as "jujutsu": "ju," which means gentleness or softness. This shared root explains the principle inherent in the two martial arts. Far from being "soft" in the conventional sense of being weak, both judo and jiujitsu use an indirect application of force to defeat an opponent in which the opponent's strength is used against him. The difference between the two disciplines lies in the second part of their names. "Jutsu" (jujutsu) simply means "science" or "techniques" of softness. The use of "do" in judo means "way" or "path" to softness, lending more philosophical overtones to the discipline.

Naming his school Kodokan Judo was deliberate on Kano's part as an effort to move away from the ancient jiujitsu teachings whose sole purpose in the end was to teach someone to kill. For Kano, judo was a means to improve yourself physically, mentally and spiritually. He saw that as Japan was changing and accepting the ways of the modern world, so too should the ancient martial arts.

Kano's style was simple, yet it was a revelation to the jiujitsu world. Jiujitsu forms had barely changed since the time of the samurai. Various schools focused on one aspect of the art or another, but the basic formulas remained the same. Tradition dictated that the forms be respected, and the old masters of jiujitsu refused to break the bonds of their medieval methodology. Kano, who was part of the new, open Japan, embraced change, and he developed a new methodology clearly superior to the old one.

Along with his new methods of throwing an opponent, Kano's major breakthrough was his perfection of putting an opponent off balance. For centuries, jiujitsu had relied on using leverage on an opponent to execute a maneuver, but Kano thought that it would be easier to throw an opponent if he was put off balance first. Although this sounds like a simple idea today, it was a brand-new concept in the jiujitsu world back then. Kano fully embraced this concept and made it central to many of his techniques. To test his new techniques, he went up against his old master and promptly threw him to the ground three times. "From now on, you teach me," his old teacher reportedly remarked.

Despite winning over a few converts, the established jiujitsu schools were still skeptical of the diminutive martial arts instructor. After all, who was this 20-something to suggest that centuries of martial arts tradition had gotten it all wrong? What Kano needed was a large-scale forum to show the world that his judo was the new powerhouse in the martial arts world. In the mid-1880s, Kano finally got the chance to prove his new style was the best when the chief of the Tokyo Metropolitan Police handpicked challengers from both schools to battle it out to decide whose martial art was the most effective. The outcome of the tournament would decide the fate of Kano's school. Kano's student won 13 out of 15 bouts and had two draws. Kano had proven that his judo was a new force in the martial arts that would be around for a long time.

Once judo achieved acceptance in Japan, Kano wanted to teach other parts of the world his new martial art. Judo, after all, was a way of life and a means of self-defense. Kano thought judo could benefit countless people throughout the world—through physical fitness, a calm, centered mind and a peaceful spirit. Kano traveled overseas to America and to Europe to spread the word about judo. He even became a member of the International Olympic Committee to promote the sport, joining in 1909.

While the lineage of Japanese-style judo continued in a direct line, changing little from the original style practiced by Kano, one of his students, Mitsuyo Maeda, would be responsible for another revolution in the world of martial arts.

The Wanderings of Mitsuyo Maeda

Fighting was a passion for Mitsuyo Maeda, and he wanted nothing more than to travel the world and show that his martial art was the best. In 1904, at the age of 26, he packed his bags and departed his native Japan for the first time. After giving a few demonstrations in the United States with some fellow judo students, Maeda parted ways with them and began to hang out with professional fighters—that is, boxers and wrestlers. The other students wanted to spread the judo philosophy to the world, but Maeda was bitten by the capitalist bug and saw the perfect opportunity to make some money with his newfound friends. He took his judo skills on the road, and in every new town, he organized a series of matches against anyone willing to take him on.

For the next several years, Maeda traveled all over the Americas and Europe, spreading the art of judo and challenging all comers. He even had the gall to challenge heavyweight boxing superstar Jack Johnson, but the fight never materialized.

After traveling the globe, Maeda found that some of his most receptive audiences were in Mexico and South America. After spending a few years in Mexico and in Cuba, he settled down in Pará, Brazil, where he continued to put on his public performances. During one of Maeda's shows, a young Carlos Gracie sat in the audience and watched in awe as the tiny Japanese man challenged and defeated every fighter who stepped into the ring. Carlos was enchanted by the power and techniques Maeda displayed in the arena, and he ran home to tell his father Gastao Gracie about what he had seen. It wasn't long after seeing Maeda's performance that Gastao, a man with connections in the business and political world, hired Maeda to give lessons to Carlos.

This relationship was how Maeda became associated with the Gracies, a family that would one day take what Maeda had shown them and forever change the fighting world.

Brazilian Inception

The first Gracie to learn Maeda's form of judo was Carlos, the eldest son of politician Gastao Gracie. Not a particularly physically imposing child, Carlos was often the target of the bigger kids at school, so Gastao thought that, considering Maeda's size compared to his toughness in a fight, Maeda could teach Carlos to defend himself.

Maeda taught Carlos many of the techniques of classical Kano-judo, but because Maeda had traveled the world and learned different techniques from wrestlers and prizefighters, he also incorporated some of those styles into his lessons. Renzo Gracie wrote about his famous ancestor's early non-traditional training in his book *Mastering Jujitsu*:

> [Maeda] *did not limit his teachings to judo. In fact, in one old photograph, Maeda is shown training without the traditional Japanese gi jacket, and it reveals him using a standard control and submission technique of Western catch wrestling: a half nelson and hammer lock. Maeda was a regular competitor in catch wrestling events while in England, and there is no doubt that he absorbed what he took to be useful from these arts and incorporated them into his training and teaching.*

Although it's unclear when Maeda began instructing Carlos, the training lasted for four years before Maeda left Pará for other towns in Brazil. But during that time, Carlos had transformed from the shy, skinny pushover to a confident young man with a well-conditioned set of fighting skills. Even without a teacher, Carlos continued to practice and eventually began to pass on what he had learned to his younger siblings: Oswaldo, Gastao Jr., Jorge and Helio. Maeda taught the young Carlos everything he could in their years together, but Carlos had barely scratched the surface of what judo had to offer.

According to his family's descriptions, Carlos had certainly learned ground-fighting techniques and classic judo throwing moves, but he never learned the advanced techniques of putting an opponent off balance. Without someone to guide the Gracie family through their training, they were left to their own devices, and out of this free training would come a new style of fighting that was eventually called Gracie jiujitsu.

In 1921, Gastao Gracie and his family moved to the big city of Rio de Janeiro. Although judo was a proper martial art sufficient for the small town of Pará, Rio was a bustling metropolis known for its high crime rates and violent machete-wielding street gangs, and judo didn't seem to have the grit that was required to survive on the streets. The Gracie family continued to develop their own fighting techniques, and by the late 1920s, they felt it was time to take their system to the public and prove that their fighting style was the best.

Opening a school of his own in the late 1920s, Carlos Gracie figured that the best way to advertise his system was to challenge any and all comers, no matter their level of training or physical size. At first, Carlos and his brothers welcomed any challengers to fight them at their schools, but they also went as far as fighting out in the streets or on the famous beaches of Rio in front of throngs of sunbathers. In this manner, the Gracie brothers quickly developed a reputation as men not to be messed with. With his confidence and bravado at a maximum, Carlos placed an ad in the local newspaper in search of new challengers. It read, "Want a broken rib? Look for Carlos Gracie."

The True Beginning of Gracie Jiujitsu

Carlos Gracie might have started the family jiujitsu dynasty, but it was his brother Helio who defined it as "Gracie jiujutsu," a contribution that would define the history of the mixed martial arts genre. Carlos had brought attention to jiujutsu from his battles in the gym and streets of

Rio de Janiero, but he had never bothered to form his fighting style into a teachable system. His remained a true *vale tudo* martial art.

VALE TUDO

Portuguese for "anything goes," *vale tudo* is a Brazilian form of fighting that developed in the early 20th century in traveling carnivals. Alongside acrobats, alligator-skin men and the bearded lady, there was the fighters booth where one or more fighters would take challenges from the crowd. Later, *vale tudo* would move to television, where martial arts men from all disciplines battled it out before a live audience.

While Carlos traveled around Brazil and challenged all comers, he left Helio back home in Rio in charge of continuing the jiujitsu school program. Carlos taught his brothers a mix of judo and wrestling techniques that he had learned from his teacher Mitsuyo Maeda. Carlos' style of fighting relied more on his size and strength rather than on the perfection of technique, but Helio was always sick as a young man and not as strong as his other brothers, which meant that many of the techniques of judo were beyond his capabilities.

However, Helio was not about to be left behind by his brothers, and sibling rivalry motivated him to adapt the art to suit

Guard position: The fighter on his back uses his legs and hips to prevent his opponent from gaining control. Two variations of the guard are the closed guard in which a fighter's legs are locked around an opponent, and the open guard, where the legs are not locked but still keep the opponent from gaining dominance on the ground.

his physical needs. The jiujitsu of Carlos was powerful, explosive and focused on the difficult throws. Helio's genius came in adapting what his brother taught him to match his abilities. He created a fighting style that was based on judo techniques but also focused on ground fighting, where a smaller opponent was on more even terms with a larger opponent. For example, Helio knew that because he was a much smaller man than most fighters, he would eventually end up on his back. In traditional judo and jiujitsu, this was not a considered a desirable position to be in, but Helio perfected different moves so that a fight could result in the guard position.

For Helio, winning was not about force but about leverage. "You, for example, cannot lift a car with the strength of your arms, but with a jack you can lift a car. That's what I did," said Helio in an interview about the creation of his style.

I discovered techniques of leverage that optimize force. These modifications made a form of jiujitsu that is superior to the jiujitsu that existed before that, and today the jiujitsu that the entire world knows is my jiujitsu.

Though for Helio, it wasn't enough to simply show in his classes that he could defeat all challengers; like Carlos before him, he actually went out into the streets to prove the new Gracie jiujitsu was superior to all other types of martial arts. Once, during a street fight, he injured his opponent so badly that he was arrested by the police and was only saved from jail when the Brazilian president stepped in and pardoned him for the offense. Helio also fought Brazil's other martial artists and wrestlers passing through from other countries, and in those fights, he usually won with ease or fought to a stalemate against much larger fighters. With such a record against opponents, Helio Gracie's name began to spread among the martial arts community, and challengers from around the world soon began knocking at his door seeking to put their skills to the Gracie test.

The Japanese Rival

One of the most legendary battles in Gracie family history was against someone many have called the greatest Japanese judo master, Masahiko Kimura. In 1935, when Kimura was 18 years old, he became the youngest person to earn a fifth-degree black belt in judo when he defeated eight consecutive opponents. He undertook a training regimen that teetered on the obsessive, reportedly doing over 1000 push-ups and practicing judo up to nine hours per day. In his professional fighting career, aside from four losses (all of which occurred in the span of one off year), Kimura was never even taken off his feet in a judo match.

After dominating the judo world for so long, he began to train in karate and wrestling techniques in pursuit of becoming an invincible fighter. But when his wife contracted tuberculosis, Kimura needed to make money to pay for her treatments. The world of judo was not the most lucrative business, so Kimura jumped into professional wrestling to help pay the bills. He signed a three-month contract with a fight promoter that saw him travel to the Hawaiian Islands in the late 1940s to give judo exhibitions and take on any local challengers foolish enough to get in the ring with him. Kimura decided to prolong his trip and agreed to a four-month stint in Brazil to give demonstrations and teach his techniques.

Kimura was making good money and did not want to ruin his new business by getting into any fights, but when Helio Gracie heard an undefeated Japanese judo master had wandered into town, he could not resist challenging the foreigner. At first, Kimura politely declined the offer, but Helio was not one to take no for an answer and kept at Kimura to fight him in an arena. It was sheer bravado on Helio's part to challenge Kimura, but he knew if he could defeat him, he would prove that Gracie jiujitsu was the most powerful martial art in the world. Initially, Kimura did not even entertain the notion of fighting Helio, but when Gracie defeated one of Kimura's students by choking him into unconsciousness, Kimura could no longer sit idly by. He now had to accept Gracie's challenge.

Kimura and Gracie would fight at Rio's brand-new Estadio do Maracana in 1951, an arena with a capacity of 200,000, but only 20,000 people showed up to see the fight. In the media, Helio was all bravado before the fight, but years later, he admitted that the odds were in fact heavily on Kimura's side. "I wasn't the only one who thought that nobody in the world could defeat Kimura," he said.

> *My brother Carlos was worried that I would never give up under any condition. He thought I would get seriously injured. So he gave me permission to fight with Kimura on the condition that I would "give up" without fail.*

Despite Helio believing that he barely had a chance to win, it did not stop him from putting on an impressive show for the crowd when he arrived at the arena, bringing with him a coffin for Kimura to be placed in once he had finished him off. Kimura simply laughed off the Brazilian's bravado.

When the opening gong sounded in the arena, it was clear who the better fighter was, as Kimura tossed Helio around the ring like a rag doll. Kimura continued to toy with Helio, putting on an exhibition of classic judo moves intending to knock out Helio with a throw, but the mats were too soft. Changing his tactics, Kimura then took the fight to the ground. Many thought this would be Helio's moment to turn the fight around, but Kimura controlled the pace by smothering Helio's face with his belly so that Helio could not breathe. It was while Helio was struggling to get out from under Kimura by lifting him off with his left hand that Kimura found his way out of the fight. Kimura explained how the fight ended in his memoir *My Judo*:

> *That moment, I grabbed his left wrist with my right hand, and twisted up his arm. I applied Udegarami* [also known as the Kimura arm lock]. *I thought he would surrender immediately. But Helio would not tap the mat. I had no choice but to keep on twisting the arm. The stadium became quiet. The bone of his arm was coming close to the breaking point. Finally, the sound of the bone breaking echoed throughout the stadium. Helio still did not surrender.*

Incredibly, neither Helio nor his corner would throw in the towel to surrender, and Kimura continued to apply pressure to Helio's arm, breaking it in another place. Still Helio did not tap out. But when Kimura went to twist his arm further, the Gracie corner finally threw in the towel and the fight was over. While Kimura's corner raised his arm in victory and paraded him

Kimura arm lock: The technique involves locking onto the opponent's arm from the mounted side control or the guard position. The arm is then cranked away from the opponent, putting pressure on the shoulder and elbow joints to the point where the arm is brought behind his back.

around the ring, Kimura happened to look over at Helio. He wrote, "Helio let his left arm hang and looked very sad withstanding the pain." Interestingly, Brazilian newspapers did not lead with the story of Helio's defeat at the hands of the Japanese judoka but with a deceptive headline that had "Vitoria de Helio Gracie" (Victory for Helio Gracie) plastered on the front in huge type—preceded by the word "Moralmente" (Moral) in much smaller type.

After the bout, Kimura traveled around for a few more years but eventually returned to his wife in Japan. There he took up a position at a university and continued to train students in judo.

Helio Gracie, however, was not completely done. After healing from his stomach-churning injuries, he retired from active competition and turned his attention to running the increasingly popular Gracie Academy. Everything was going smoothly in the world of Gracie martial arts, but one of his school instructors thought he could turn his talents into cash by joining the professional wrestling circuit. Helio was adamant that his students or teachers not use what they had learned in such an arena as wrestling, which he found to be disrespectful to all martial arts and to his school in particular. However, one instructor, Waldemar Santana, did not heed his master's words and performed in a wrestling match, even going as far as insulting his former school in the local newspaper. When Gracie demanded that Santana apologize for his comments, Santana refused, and Helio was forced to challenge his former student to a fight to uphold the honor of his name and his academy. The fight was a battle of artful technicians that lasted over three hours before Santana knocked a tired Gracie out cold with a kick to the head.

Although the losses to Kimura and one of his former students were tough to accept, the Gracie brand of martial arts by then was firmly established on the streets of Rio de Janiero as the most effective method of self-defense. Helio had taken what his brother had taught him and turned it into a fighting method that has become an essential tool in the modern mixed martial arts fighter's arsenal. But more importantly, Helio shared his knowledge with all of his nine children, who then took what their father had shown them and made the Gracie name a worldwide phenomenon.

HELIO GRACIE OFFSPRING

Helio Gracie was a man with a lot of energy, which he used to defeat opponents as well as father nine children by two wives. His first marriage produced three sons: Rickson, Rorion and Relson. With his second wife, he had four more sons (Royler, Rolker, Royce and Robin) and two daughters (Rerika and Ricci).

The Gracie Legacy Spreads

While the Gracies had been established in Brazil for decades, and their fighting style was proven as the most effective martial art on the streets and beaches of Rio de Janeiro, the greater world knew nothing of the power of Gracie jiujitsu. In the 1970s, all of what the world knew of martial arts they saw in Bruce Lee movies and the karate films of Sonny Chiba. But for the Gracie family and their followers, kung fu and karate might look good on film, but in a real fight, fighters would not stand a chance against the Gracie method. Most members of the Gracie family were more than content with staying in Brazil and playing in the sun and sand, except for Rorion Gracie.

Being a star in Brazil was one thing, but Rorion believed that the world needed to know about Gracie jiujitsu, and to make it anywhere, he felt he first needed to make it in the U.S. So in 1978, Rorion departed for the U.S. to seek his fortune and spread the message of Gracie jiujitsu.

Rorion, like many others before him with a great idea and tons of enthusiasm, arrived in Los Angeles and expected to be welcomed with open arms. Despite the benefits that Gracie jiujitsu offered, Rorion had trouble convincing a wider audience of the sport's merits.

For 10 years, while teaching a few students in a small gym, Rorion flipped burgers, cleaned houses and worked in gardens to make ends meet, and he never stopped believing that he had a golden idea for the world.

During that decade, his brothers Rickson, Royler and Royce joined him in Los Angeles, and with his brothers to back him up, Rorion knew he had to do something different to get people's attention. Rorion and his brothers accepted challenges from anybody to prove the superiority of the Gracie method. Opponents from the traditional martial arts showed up at the Gracie dojo (Rorion's garage) one after the other and would invariably go home defeated and confused at how these Brazilians could defeat them so easily.

Rorion did not have to fight in his garage much longer, however, because he had caught the eye of a television producer who got him small roles in TV shows and movies. With the increased notoriety and an increase in student enrollment, Rorion was finally able to move out of his garage and open up an academy of his own. But he was not satisfied with simply having his own jiujitsu academy; Rorion wanted to take his sport to another level. His idea was to take his brand of martial arts onto a stage like no one had ever seen in North America, an arena where fighters from all backgrounds could test their skills against the world's best in different fields. Rorion's family already had experience in organizing something similar back in the 1930s and '40s when Carlos and Helio had fought in the *vale tudo*. The trick was in selling their brand of fighting to an American audience.

In the Land of the Rising Sun

If you know the enemy and know yourself, you need not fear the result of a hundred battles. If you know yourself but not the enemy, for every victory gained you will also suffer a defeat. If you know neither the enemy nor yourself, you will succumb in every battle.

—Sun Tzu, *Art of War*

The ultimate value of life depends upon awareness, and the power of contemplation rather than upon mere survival.

—Aristotle

Practice is not a matter of years and months. It is a matter of concentration.

—Koichi Tohei

While the Gracie family was busy developing their own style of fighting in Brazil and in the United States, in Japan, the world of MMA fighting continued to evolve separately but toward the same end.

World War II had practically destroyed most of Japan, and its people had the daunting task not only of rebuilding their infrastructure but also of dealing with the total reconstruction of themselves. Throwing off decades of imperialism might not seem like an easy task, but the Japanese had proven in the past to be a culture adept at change while remaining unique. The rebuilding process after the war was difficult, but the new generation rising out of the ashes looked upon the world as a new place to explore and to synthesize with their own.

The biggest influence on the new emerging Japanese culture was the United States. After Japan surrendered in the war, the U.S. occupied the country from 1945 to 1952, but the cultural ties between its people continued beyond the arbitrary political dates.

One of the most popular distinctly American cultural legacies that got passed on to the Japanese was wrestling. This was not the wrestling of the Greco-Roman tradition but a unique American creation that pushed the wrestlers into a role of actors more than athletes. Yet even with determined outcomes and prepared shows, the Japanese simply loved wrestling. In a country troubled with soaring prices, food scarcity and high unemployment, wrestling provided an outlet for people to vent their frustrations. Some of the most popular wrestlers of the day in Japan were the ones who routinely fought and defeated bigger American challengers, giving nationalists something to cheer about, at least for a few hours. The most popular wrestler in postwar Japan was without a doubt the legendary Rikidozan.

The years following the war were a boon time for Rikidozan's popularity, but as the 1960s approached, and Japan began to emerge out of the rubble as the world's new technological giant, wrestling seemed less important to the population. Looking for new ways to attract fans, Rikidozan moved away from beating on American challengers and took on a more traditional Japanese warrior. In a famous example of the mixing of fighting disciplines, Rikidozan took on the famed judo master Masahiko Kimura, and although the fight was clearly predetermined, fans loved the idea of pitting two different martial art disciplines against one another. Watching that match from the sidelines was Rikidozan's young protégé, Antonio Inoki.

Passing the Torch

Born in 1943 to a wealthy family in the city of Yokohama, Japan, Kanji Inoki was a gifted athlete from a very early age. His first introduction to the martial arts came in the sixth grade when his brother taught him karate, but Kanji's interests were diverse, and he later joined the basketball team and the track and field team in high school. But life in Japan in the 1950s was not easy, and the once affluent Inoki family fell on hard times. To find work and a new life, the family moved to Brazil.

It was in Brazil that Kanji took on the name Antonio and where the promising track and field athlete met Japanese wrestling legend Rikidozan. After only four years in Brazil, Inoki returned to his native country with Rikidozan and other wrestlers. Under the tutelage of Rikidozan, Inoki learned all he could from the master wrestler and showman. But as wrestling began its decline in Japan in the 1960s, Inoki recognized that if wanted to continue his passion for putting on a show, his art would have to change with the times.

Searching for a new idea to bring to the public, Inoki remembered that one fight Rikidozan had with the famed judoka Kimura. However, still in the shadow of his famous teacher, Inoki could not strike out on his own. He remained in his mentor's shadow for several years, wrestling in secondary matches, but he could never break out to the top. Everything changed in 1963 when Rikidozan was murdered at the hands of the Japanese mafia, the yakuza, reportedly because of a fight in a club with one of its members. This incident left Inoki the biggest wrestling star in Japan.

After fighting in various wrestling associations from 1963 to 1971 and never settling into a role in any of them because of behind-the-scenes fighting, Inoki decided it was time to start a wrestling association of his own that would once and for all prove that wrestling was the most effective of all fighting arts and that his fighters could defeat all comers of any discipline and size.

In 1972, Inoki founded New Japan Pro Wrestling, whose mission was to be a place where fighters of all backgrounds could compete. Despite the outcomes being largely predetermined, the idea of a giving a forum for different styles of martial arts to fight before a crowd had its genesis in the New Japan Pro Wrestling. Wrestling historian Hisaharu Tanabe, in the book *Total MMA* by author Jonathan Snowden, said, "Many people criticize Inoki for constantly 'mixing up' pro wrestling and MMA. However, if you look back at the history, you just can't avoid the connection between those two sports...at least in Japan."

Those early fights of New Japan Pro Wrestling with Inoki versus athletes such as famed wrestler Karl Gotch and Olympic judo gold medalist Wilheim Ruska may seem tame and completely staged, but Inoki displayed proper fighting techniques in his matches and never made his performance against a fighter look easy. One of the most memorable moments in Inoki's wrestling career was in a fight against the eccentric 6-foot-4-inch, 465-pound Canadian strongman, Antonio Barichievich, aka "The Great Antonio."

During the bout, the Great Antonio drifted away from the script of the fight and landed a series of blows to Inoki that got the Japanese fighter more than a little upset. Inoki proceeded to smack the Canadian giant with several severe open-hand blows to his opponent's face before putting him to the ground, where he repeatedly kicked and stomped his face into a bloody mess that was certainly not part of the scripted outcome.

These fights, however, were still considered traditional wrestling matches, and if Inoki wanted to prove to the world that wrestling was the greatest style of fighting, he would have to take on an opponent of far greater stature. The bout would be the greatest fight of his life and the first time a MMA fight was broadcast on a global scale.

Inoki versus Ali

Muhammad Ali was never one to keep his mouth shut. If he had something to say, he made sure the world heard it. In 1975, during an interview with the Japanese *Sankei Sports* newspaper, Ali lamented the lack of a challenger from the Far East to take him on in the ring. This comment was nothing more than sheer bravado on Ali's part, giving the media what they had expected to come out of his mouth. There was no doubt that Ali immediately forgot all about that insignificant interview, but Antonio Inoki read every word and took it to heart.

For more than a year, Inoki made it his goal to fight against Ali, and he used tactics that Ali was familiar with, such as calling Ali out in the press to challenge him and even going as far as distributing pamphlets that read, "Ali, Don't Run Away!"

Ali had long been a fan of professional wrestling, and after giving the idea some thought, he finally gave in to Inoki's demands and agreed to fight. At first, it was Ali's understanding that the bout would play out like a regular wrestling match—fake moves, predetermined outcome and completely harmless. Even in the lead-up to the fight, Ali played up the fight like a pro wrestler. "This will be serious," he said during the press conference announcing the fight. "This will be a fight to the death. No boxing. This will be on the level." Even Ali's manager, "Classy" Freddie Blassie, chimed into the fray adding, "It shall not be no Pearl Harbor! Muhammad Ali has returned! Just like MacArthur! He shall destroy him!"

The fight was an odd venue for the boxing legend, but Ali appeared to relish the opportunity to try something different and make close to $6 million in the process. To Ali, the match would proceed as follows: he would pummel Inoki throughout the match before finally beating him down to the mat where Inoki might then cut his forehead to draw blood and collapse in defeat. Then as Ali turned away in victory, Inoki would rise from behind and knock Ali out with a kick to the head. Ali would "lose" the fight, but it would be patently obvious to everyone watching who was the better man. Ali would receive his money, and Inoki would become the most famous wrestler in the world. This was how things were supposed to work, but the event turned out completely different.

Despite Inoki's reputation as a wrestler of predetermined fights when Ali signed on to the match, Ali received a severe bashing from critics. Japanese newspapers were furious that the great Muhammad Ali would sink to such a level after openly stating that he could beat any Asian challengers.

Stateside, the press was not that forgiving either. The *New York Times* wrote, "Boxing is show business. Maybe it's unrealistic to expect more of a champion than a succession of pratfalls on the burlesque circuit. Nevertheless, some do mourn for the sweet science."

With all of the negative press leading up to the event, Ali and his advisors decided that going through with the fake fight would do more harm than good.

BRAIN HICCUP

In an ironic twist to the fight between Muhammad Ali and Antonio Inoki, the person who was charged with promoting the first global MMA fight, "Big" Bob Arum, was the same man who some 30 years later would make a racist comment about the intended audience and say other derogatory statements, such as people just don't want to see "guys rolling around on the ground like homosexuals."

Days before the June 26, 1976, scheduled fight, Ali and his camp insisted that the fight be a real one. The only problem was that there had never been a big MMA fight before, and neither Ali's people nor Inoki's knew how to arrange the fight. Not a trained boxer, would Inoki don boxing gloves and attempt to fight the greatest boxer of his time? Would Ali remove his gloves and meet Inoki on his turf? The final rules of the match were not agreed on until a few hours before the fight. Having invested so much time and money into the event, the Japanese were forced to give the advantage to Ali, and the final rules were a surprise to no one; they were heavily in the Champ's favor.

It was decided that there would be no take-downs below the waist; Inoki, who would not be wearing boxing gloves, was not allowed to throw punches or make kicks to Ali's head or body; and if Inoki happened to get Ali on the ground, he was not allowed to throw punches. However, it was highly unlikely that Ali would let Inoki get close enough for an upper body takedown maneuver, so all Inoki was left with against the greatest heavyweight boxer was really a simple leg kick, and even that kick was hindered with the rule that he could kick only if he was down on one knee. With such restrictive rules, Inoki believed he could still defeat Ali in the ring, and he agreed to the rulings despite the prospect of the fight being a complete farce.

From the outset of the match, spectators in the arena and others watching at home knew they would not see the average fight spectacle. Inoki stood in one corner of the ring wearing his tight, black wrestling shorts while Ali entered the ring in loose, white boxing trunks. The image didn't look right; it was like one of them had walked into the wrong ring. The bell finally sounded after the introductions, and thus began 15 rounds of one of the strangest fights in history. The only thing Inoki could do to survive was to drop onto the mat on all fours or sit on his behind and scamper around the ring kicking at Ali's legs. Even though Inoki seemed to be at a disadvantage, he was able to use his one weapon in that position and repeatedly kicked at Ali's leg throughout the bout. Ali landed five punches in over 40 minutes of fighting while Inoki connected with over 50 kicks to the champ's legs and dropped Ali several times.

But despite Inoki's superior performance and adaptation to the restrictive rules, the officials called the bout a draw. In truth, Inoki had come out of the fight after 15 rounds with barely a scratch, while Ali was forced to go to the hospital after the event. Promoter Bob Arum described the frustration of the event for the Ali camp best: "Finally, at the end of the 15th round, the referee calls it a draw. So fine, okay. It was terrible. It was embarrassing. But Ali is bleeding from the legs. He gets an infection in his legs; almost has to have an amputation.... Ali could've been a cripple for the rest of his life."

At the outset, Inoki's goal was to gain international acclaim, but instead, the fight brought him nothing but criticism. Ali suffered physically, and his reputation had been damaged, but the world quickly forgot he had ever been in this bout once he scheduled another fight. Regardless its shady rules and rough execution, the match brought attention to a new potential in prizefighting. Promoters and fighters alike began to realize that the public would pay to see fighters of different disciplines

ANTONIO INOKI

Antonio Inoki tried again to capture international attention when he announced a wrestling match against Ugandan dictator Idi Amin, but that event was cancelled when the dictator was overthrown. While still wrestling, Inoki even entered into Japanese politics. During the Gulf War, he met with Saddam Hussein to negotiate the release of Japanese prisoners. Saddam was a big wrestling fan and gave Inoki a pair of golden swords as a gift.

square off in the ring, and within a few short years, innovators began the first tentative steps into the mixed martial arts world.

A Brief Visit to the USA

While an appetite for "real" wrestling had been created in Japan, in the United States, wrestling fans had fully embraced the theatrical side of the sport with the rise of the World Wrestling Federation (WWF) and stars like Hulk Hogan and Andre the Giant. Although not taking away any of the athletic ability of the wrestlers in the WWF, the brand of wrestling they offered the public was and still is a theater performance. Yet even with ridiculous premises and even more ridiculous spectacles, fans ate it up. Some wrestlers in Japan openly laughed at the comical nature of American wrestling, but its popularity was on the rise in the land of the rising sun. Hulk Hogan and Andre the Giant even made the long trip to Tokyo in the mid-1980s to battle it out with Japan's most famous wrestler, Antonio Inoki, to seize on the growing popularity of glamour wrestling.

With this more American-style wrestling beginning to creep into the Japanese circuit, certain members of Japan's established association, the New Japan Pro Wrestling, took offense to the theatrical style in their realm. Japanese wrestling transplant Karl Gotch, Akira Maeda, Yoshiaki Fujiwara and others all quit the club and went out on their own to try to get the public to see their vision for a new style of fighting.

Rings Fighting Network

The first person to envision a real future for the sport of mixed martial arts was Akira Maeda. After spending years fighting in the professional wrestling circuit, Maeda had become disillusioned with his sport. For Maeda and many of his contemporary athletes, the over-the-top moves, garish costumes, leaps from turnbuckles and the use of props, such as steel chairs, was a distressing trend in their beloved sport that they viewed as a form of art. For these men, fighting was real, and they believed that if fans were promised a real fight without all the gimmicks, they would pay good money to see it over and over again.

Despite the potential of a pure fighting association, Maeda needed to test the public's desire for real mixed martial arts fighting. Under the banner of the Universal Wrestling Federation, an event was scheduled on November 29, 1989, at the Tokyo Dome that promised wrestling fans something they had never seen before.

Tickets sold out in less than a week. The fans believed at first they were getting the real thing. The fights were without a doubt predetermined, but the actions between the wrestlers were real. None of the fighters held back with their kicks, and open-hand slaps were fast and loud. Most importantly, each fighter stayed true to the techniques of his respective martial art, whether it was wrestling or judo, and each fight was filled with arm bars, choke holds and hip throws.

Some of the fans were disappointed by the fixed bouts, but most who had seen the fights walked away enthusiastic about the future of mixed martial arts. However, the Universal Wrestling Federation did not last long; internal bickering between the wrestlers saw it fold in 1991.

Although the first baby steps into the world of mixed martial arts in Japan turned out to be a failure, it gave Akira Maeda the opportunity he wanted to break away from the pack and start a new venture of his own. In May 1991, Maeda formed the fighting network, Rings. For Maeda, this network would not be a group of fighters or a system of promotion—he wanted to take mixed martial arts fighting to a worldwide audience. The potential for this type of event was there, but Maeda was trying to build a global sports organization that did not have a legitimate history in any country. But Maeda was determined, and he traveled the world setting up networks of fighters, which were particularly successful in Holland and Russia.

Maeda now had to get a media outlet to agree to broadcast his fights. The only issue was that no one, including the fans, wanted to see a group of unknown fighters battle it out in the ring. Maeda was the star attraction, and if he wanted to get his fights broadcast, he had to suit up. This created a tough position for the aging Maeda. He wanted to move his new federation toward real fights, but at 34 years of age, Maeda could not participate in those fights. What occurred in the Rings fights was that the undercard fights had competitive bouts while the top fighters were usually involved in scripted matches. The Rings fights saw some early success with the Japanese public, but the network's reliance on Maeda would lead to its ultimate demise.

After participating in a few fights as the drawing card, Maeda's age eventually caught up with him when he injured his knee to the point where he could barely walk by early 1993. It was around this time that other MMA associations began springing up in Japan and around the world. Then in November 1993, the UFC made its debut in North America. The popularity of the no-holds-barred fighting suddenly made the Rings fights seem ridiculous and antiquated to fighting fans. Given the option, fans began moving over by the thousands to the more raw fighting of other Japanese wrestling organizations such as Pancrase, K-1 and eventually Pride. Rings lasted a few more years by trying to incorporate more of the real fighting, but every fighter they brought through the ranks was eventually signed to bigger fight networks like Pancrase and Pride. Rings folded operations in 2002, but it left its mark as one of the first fighting networks to promote mixed martial arts.

Pancrase

Japanese Pancrase truly was where modern mixed martial arts began. No longer were fights predetermined or choreographed in any way. Fans wanted the real thing—to see wrestler versus judo artist, and jiujitsu versus Greco-Roman. The previous incarnations of the sport had flirted with displays of martial arts prowess, but they all fell victim to the old theatrical mentality that had permeated wrestling for decades. Rings had tried to bring true martial arts fighting to the greater public, but the attempt had failed after the organization bowed to pressure from television networks to incorporate "fake" wrestling into its "real" programs. Two of Japan's most famous wrestling stars had finally had enough of the farce and decided to start their own wrestling league in 1993.

Masakatsu Funaki and Minoru Suzuki wanted to take wrestling back to its roots. To them, wrestling had become a joke, far removed from its glorious history since the time of the ancient Greeks. It would be a risky venture because the two wrestlers had already made names for themselves in the traditional pro wrestling circuits, but the two men remained true to their training and were not looking to perform on the stage like comedians or clowns in the way that their counterparts in America were doing on a weekly basis in the WWF. Funaki and Suzuki felt that if the public were given the opportunity to see what real wrestling matches were about, they would eventually create legions of fans.

This "real" fighting had been sold to the Japanese wrestling fans before. Antonio Inoki had wrestled martial artists in bouts that had been promoted as the real thing. The UWF had even incorporated wrestling techniques and holds that were designed to look realistic, though the matches were anything but authentic. Funaki and Suzuki wanted to go all the way with the idea of real fights in which outcomes were decided purely by the quality and determination of the fighter.

Funaki and Suzuki decided that the matches in their fights would be based on modified wrestling rules. The rules were:

- No elbows to the head (neither while standing nor on the ground).

- No closed-fist strikes to the head (neither while standing nor on the ground).

- No knees to the head on the ground.

- No kicks or stomps to the head on the ground.

- If a participant gets too close to the ropes, he is stood back up on his feet at the same spot (as opposed to Pride's rule of re-centering to the middle of the ring.)

- Non-title matches consist of one 15-minute round, while title matches consist of one 30-minute round.

- If a participant is caught in a submission and taps out, it is a loss.

- Five "escapes" are given to each fighter at the start of every match. An escape can be used when caught in a submission near the ropes, in which case the participant can grab them, be stood back on his feet and have one point deducted. Once a participant has used all of his escapes, it is a loss.

- For knockouts, a 10 count similar to boxing and kickboxing is used. If the participant is unable to answer the 10 count, the fight is declared a TKO and that fighter loses the match. However, if the participant is able to answer the 10 count, the fight resumes and one point is deducted from that fighter's point total.

- If, at the end of regulated time, neither fighter has submitted, has been knocked out or has lost all his points, a decision is rendered based on which fighter lost fewer points. If neither fighter lost any points, or both have lost the same number of points, the fight is declared a draw.

Although the idea seemed simple, critics predicted the wrestling league would fail in a matter of months if not faster. Funaki and Suzuki were popular, but they could not base the entire network of fights and promotions only around themselves as had Akira Maeda and his Rings network. The two innovators needed to create their own supply of popular wrestlers and turn them into stars.

One of the first famous wrestlers to join the Pancrase circuit was Ken Shamrock.

Shamrock had previously fought in the Universal Fighting Championship alongside Suzuki and Funaki and later in the Pro Wrestling Fujiwara Gumi. A big man wrapped in thick muscle, and with a scowl that would scare the toughest fighters, Shamrock became a fast favorite in the world of Japanese pro wrestling, but like Funaki and Suzuki, he craved a greater challenge.

The problem for the new Pancrase fighters was that guys like Shamrock, Funaki and Suzuki were too good, and fights often lasted only a few minutes. To create new stars in the circuit, the veterans of fighting would intentionally lose matches to lesser opponents to make the fights more entertaining. Yet while the fights remained pure to the roots of wrestling and offered fans an alternative to the scripted affairs on the pro wrestling circuit, Pancrase seemed a little too refined for fans.

At the first Pancrase event held on September 21, 1993, in Tokyo, only 7000 people showed up to see Shamrock defeat his friend and mentor Funaki by using an arm triangle choke. Despite drawing big names like Shamrock and Funaki, the future of Pancrase changed once fans saw the first Ultimate Fighting Championship held in November 1993.

Triangle choke: A technique found in judo and Brazilian jiujitsu, in which the attacker positions his arms so that he traps his opponent's head and single arm using his own arm and the opponent's to cut off blood to the brain.

All the rules created by Pancrase formed a reputable structure that assured fans of a legitimate and fair competition, but in light of the all-out bare-knuckle brawl in the UFC, Pancrase began to look tame. Pancrase required skill and technique to fight and win, while the UFC offered unbridled, no-holds-barred fistfights that appealed to people's simple, animalistic desires. Pancrase didn't stand a chance. On top of the competition from the UFC, Pancrase also had to deal with another organization in Japan that sprang up and stole all its talented fighters.

The peak moment in Pancrase history came in 1996 when Dutch-born kickboxer Bas Rutten took on the man who had introduced him into the promotion and had taught him everything he could about submission wrestling: Masakatsu Funaki. Had the two men done battle when Rutten was a rookie in the sport in 1993, Funaki would surely have beaten him with his superior grappling and wrestling skills, but by 1996, Funaki was a tired and aging superstar, and Rutten had learned much in that time. Throughout the fight, the veteran Funaki seemed to want to take the fight to the ground, but Rutten was able to stay on his feet and repeatedly smacked Funaki with devastating open-hand palm strikes and knees to the face that left the Japanese fighter bloody and dazed. Rutten ended the fight by grabbing Funaki by the neck and hitting him flush on the nose with a flying knee. After that fight, Funaki fought less and less, and with his departure, so went the luster of Pancrase.

"In the UFC it was closed fist, bare-knuckle. And no rules. It was a huge difference from Pancrase...it was a lot more strategic and you had to be a lot more skilled in your submission game. The UFC was less skilled, but a lot more danger- ous than Pancrase," said Ken Shamrock in the excellent book *The MMA Encyclopedia* by Jona- than Snowden and Kendall Shields.

With the arrival of Pride and the UFC onto the global mixed martial arts fighting scene, Pancrase found it increasingly difficult to sur- vive. Despite having big names in the MMA world like Bas Rutten, Shamrock and Guy Mezger, the audience for their brand of fighting quickly began to dwindle. In addition, Pancrase could barely hold on to their promising talent because whenever Pride or the UFC came call- ing with offers of better money and bigger audi- ences, it was impossible for the small Japanese promoters to keep their fighters.

The popular Japanese wrestlers were begin- ning to wear down as well. By the late 1990s, both Funaki and Suzuki left the ring and con- centrated on promoting the fights instead.

Amazingly, Pancrase has been able to continue operations in the form of a monthly show, but in relation to the UFC and other fight promotions, it is of marginal importance. However, there was a brief time when some of the world's most talented mixed martial artists flocked to the Pancrase arena.

Pride Fighting Championships

In the early 1990s in Japan, Nobuhiko Takada was one of the most popular and loved wrestlers in the country. He had spent a career jumping off ropes, clothes lining opponents and submitting them for a quick three count by the referee. These matches, of course, were all part of the theater of professional wrestling and were fun to watch, but with the rise of "real" fighting networks such as Rings and Pancrase, many people in Japan began to question whether their champion of professional wrestling would be able to handle himself in a proper hand-to-hand, flesh-pounding battle until one winner was left standing.

Takada had flirted with MMA in the past to give his brand of wrestling the edge that many fans were craving after their first taste of blood and gore in UFC 1. Takada even took on noted fighter and UFC tough guy Dan Severn in an attempt to add a "real" quality to his fights, and it worked. Fans seemed to eat it up. Never one to disappoint, Takada looked around the world for the toughest fighters to go up against. After a short search, he found the man he would fight next: Rickson Gracie.

Rickson had made his mark in the ring by fighting all over the world and was one of the toughest men in the business. He was exactly the type of fighter Takada and his brand of wrestling needed to legitimize the sport in the eyes of fans craving a more violent spectacle.

Takada's company, the Union of Wrestling Forces International (UWFI), approached Gracie and made him a substantial offer to fight in two matches against Takada, with both men coming out with one victory each. It was a sensible offer that the UWFI felt would leave both men with honor and a substantial paycheck.

ALL HAIL THE KING

Rickson Gracie was the toughest member of the Gracie generation that brought their brand of jiujitsu to the world. While growing up, Rickson lacked experience in the MMA tournaments that would prove his toughness; it was on the streets in Rio de Janeiro that his name became well known. His most infamous moment happened while still in Brazil when he slapped a rival on Ipanema Beach and forced him to say, "Rickson is King."

But Gracie was not about fighting with a script in his hands and declined the offer outright. The refusal did not deter UWFI promoter Yukoh Miyato, who decided that something drastic had to be done to get Gracie to fight. Miyato's idea was to send tough wrestler Yoji Anjo to Gracie's gym in California and challenge him to a fight, hopefully embarrassing the Brazilian in the process. Instead, Gracie severely beat Anjo into a bloody mess, which delivered a fatal blow to the UWFI. The organization folded not too long after the incident in 1996, having left its honor in a pool of blood on Gracie's gym floor.

This public shaming of those connected to Takada left the wrestling star in a very difficult position. His choice was either to return to the world of professional scripted wrestling or jump head first into the new sport that was sweeping across the globe. To get back his credibility and the honor of his beaten comrade, Takada officially challenged Gracie to a real fight. Gracie accepted, and the fight was scheduled for October 11, 1997, before a sold-out crowd at the Tokyo Dome.

Throughout his career, Takada had been promoted as one of the toughest fighters in professional wrestling. His legs kicks were said to be powerful enough to chop down trees and his grappling skills so refined that he could take on the greatest fighters in the world. Finally, his well-lauded talents would be put to the test.

What took Takada a career to build, Gracie destroyed in five minutes—and all it took was an arm bar. Although Takada's career had tanked, and many left the Tokyo Dome disappointed, both Kakutougi Revolution Spirits and Dream Stage Entertainment, the companies that helped stage the fight, recognized that the event was a complete marketing success and that the fans wanted more. The opportunity was there, and it was shortly after the Tokyo Dome event that the Pride Fighting Championships began, in 1997.

Pride would be different from anything the Japanese audience had ever seen. While other fighting networks, Pancrase and Rings included, were geared more toward the professional wrestling style, Pride based its appeal around the style of the Ultimate Fighting Championship that was causing a media storm in North America. Gone were the shin pads of Pancrase and the over-the-top theatrics of Rings. Pride was to be a showcase for the new modern fighter, where skill dominated showmanship and audiences could be (almost) guaranteed authentic fights. But unlike the original UFC that promoted itself as no rules, bareknuckle fighting, Pride set out a structure to ensure safety and fairness, a model that the UFC would one day follow. On the not-allowed list in Pride were:

- Head butting (enacted during Pride 12)

- Biting

- Eye gouging

- Hair pulling

- Fish hooking

- Attacks to the groin

- Strikes to the back of the head, which includes the occipital region and the spine. (The sides of the head and the area around the ears are not considered to be the back of the head.)

- Small joint manipulation (i.e., fingers and toes)

- Elbow strikes to the head and face

- Intentionally throwing your opponent out of the ring

- Running out of the ring

- Purposely holding the ropes. Fighters who purposely hang an arm or leg on the ropes will be given an immediate warning.

If you think that these rules made the Pride fights tame and handcuffed the athletes from displaying their full potential, you would be greatly mistaken. Pride was fine with a fighter stomping on the head of a downed opponent and would not stop or sanction a fighter who slammed an opponent onto the mat on his head or neck. Oh, yes, and full kicks and knees to the head of a downed opponent were kosher as well. In comparison with Pride's predecessors, this was the most violent fighting, outside Yakuza-style gang warfare, Japan had ever seen.

In the early days of the Pride championships, the monthly fights were forgettable at best and downright shameful at the worst. In Japan, the world of professional wrestling and mixed martial arts competitions were one and the same in the minds of the fans. The idea of having a fighter solely trained as an MMA fighter had yet to be conceived. Japan's best pro wrestlers continued to fall in the ring when challenged by the best the world had to offer. Takada had lost all incentive to fight in Pride, and aging star Akira Maeda was injured more often than not. In an effort to get fighters into their arenas, Pride was forced to pay a heavy price and import foreign talent. This desperation to attract fans meant that Pride organizers were not above fixing fights to have a more crowd-appealing finale.

Pride needed Takada to return to form and serve the function of drawing more fans to the sport. Takada had lost his luster in his embarrassing loss to Rickson Gracie, so Pride staged a comeback fight for the Japanese superstar against the unknown but physically imposing American fighter Kyle Sturgeon on June 24, 1998. Takada easily won the fight, but anyone witnessing the sham could clearly see that it was a staged fight.

American fans of prize fighting were livid over the outcome and for having been sold a real fight and receiving the complete opposite. Out of loyalty, Japanese fight fans took the bait and returned to Takada's corner in support. Looking to redeem himself, Takada offered up another public challenge to Gracie, who responded, "I feel Takada is a warrior and deserves the chance to try and redeem himself."

The result of that fight was quite predictable, considering Gracie's talents versus Takada's. In the fight, Takada looked like an amateur standing weak-kneed in the ring against the cool confidence of Rickson Gracie. Again, it took Gracie close to five minutes to put Takada into an arm bar and end the fight via tap out.

Arm bar: The attacker gains control of his opponent's arm, extends it out by grabbing onto the wrist and uses his body as a fulcrum to hyperextend the elbow and shoulder sockets.

With his tail firmly between his legs, Takada was no longer the impressive public figure he once was. To survive in the market, Pride tried desperately to get Takada back into the public's good graces by staging a fight with former UFC champion Mark Coleman. The results of the bout were not well received in the press, and Takada faded permanently out of mixed martial arts.

After the gross mishandling of the Takada years, Pride as an organization was in desperate need of an overhaul or they would risk losing public support. While the foreign fight fans had plenty of criticism to heap onto Pride, organizers knew that the Japanese fan was paramount, and that in Japan, fighting had always been tied directly to pro wrestling. Japanese fans had come to expect a type of narrative behind the fights they wanted to see. They liked to think of the fighters in terms of good versus bad and had a hard time simply watching two fighters pummel each other for no real reason. As bad as Takada's fixed fights had hurt the image of Pride among the Japanese and especially with the foreign audience, the fact remained that they needed a star to sell the sport. But this time around they made sure the star could actually fight. Enter into the Pride ring Kazushi Sakuraba.

Sakuraba was exactly what Pride needed to elevate the fighting events to spectacles. He was able to marshal all the flair and theatrics of a professional wrestler and had the submission grappling talent to match the legendary Gracie family. He first began to get noticed in Pride 3 when he matched grappling skills in the ring against Canadian newcomer Carlos Newton. The fight mainly took place on the mat, but it was still exciting to watch for anyone interested in the art aspect of fighting. Both fighters pushed and grabbed for position like they were playing a game of chess, with one moving into position

Knee bar: A fighter attempts to hyperextend his opponent's knee by using his arms and body position to stretch the joint to the extreme.

to execute while the other blocked and counter attacked. Eventually it was Sakuraba who came out the victor when he put Newton in a painful knee bar and forced him to tap out.

The myth of the unstoppable Japanese wrestling star had returned, and with that came the interest of the North American fight fans who found it increasingly difficult to see any form of local mixed martial arts; from 1997 till about 2002, several U.S. states banned the fights and pay-per-view refused to televise the events.

Pride became the number one ultimate fighting league, and Sakuraba was its poster boy.

Although Sakuraba lacked the flair in the ring that made Akira Maeda and Nobuhiko Takada famous, he made up for it in talent and innovation. Not satisfied with the normal arsenal of grappling and striking techniques, Sakuraba simply invented his own, much to the delight of fans. He used moves such as the flying stomp, cartwheel guard passes (literally cartwheeling over a downed opponent and landing on top of him) and the incredibly effective pro-wrestling-style karate chops. The MMA world had never seen a fighter like Sakuraba before. He had the skill of a professional grappler in the same category of the Gracie family, with innovative moves no one had seen.

With the global mixed martial arts community now firmly focused on Pride wrestling during the time the UFC was settling its image problems in North America, and with its new rising star Sakuraba, some of the best fighters in the world now flocked to Japan to prove their toughness. The first fighters of note to come calling were from the notorious Gracie family. The first to challenge Sakuraba would be technical specialist Royler Gracie, and their battle was set to take place on November 21, 1999, at Pride 8.

Although weighing in at a little over 150 pounds, former Brazilian jiujitsu world champion Royler Gracie was not someone to take lightly in the ring. By the turn of the millennium, the Gracie name had become synonymous with victories on the mixed martial arts circuits, and when Sakuraba stepped into the ring, he was the one considered the underdog, even on his home turf.

"I have nothing to prove to anyone. I have, however, a great desire to test myself. I really wanted to fight Sakuraba, not only because he is heavier than me, but also because he is such a good fighter and strategist," said Royler. "I wanted to find out how I was going to behave against a larger opponent of such a high caliber."

Royler Gracie was smart in not underestimating his opponent. Sakuraba dominated the entire length of the fight, continually blocking Royler's attempts to take the fight down to the mat and engage in a grappling skill test. Sakuraba instead used his longer reach to deliver repeated strikes to Royler's head and used devastating leg kicks to wear down his opponent. Over 25 minutes later, Sakuraba felt he had worn down his opponent enough to engage him on the ground, and he finally finished him off with a Kimura arm lock.

But Sakuraba's victory was not without its controversy. Royler had never tapped out. The referee decided to stop the fight when it appeared that Sakuraba was about to break his arm, but Royler had been blessed with extreme flexibility and after the fight said that he was never in pain. The Gracie corner refused to take the loss sitting down and strongly complained about the decision. Sakuraba was never one to get upset or disrespect his opponents after beating them, but in this instance, he spoke out to the crowd and more directly to the Gracies:

> I kind of suspected he was going to complain after the fight. But I didn't know what to say or do, or how to react.... I was thinking, "Okay, you didn't tap out, but how come you couldn't escape?" So I told the audience I would like to fight his brother Rickson, please.

However, Rickson did not want to take up Sakuraba's challenge, so it was left to the most famous Gracie at the time, Royce, to defend the family honor. The two fighters faced off at Pride Grand Prix, the organization's premiere event in 2000.

This was the battle everyone had gathered to see. Gracie did not look like much of a fighter but had proven himself to be an incredible grappling tactician ever since the world had first seen him in 1993 at UFC 1. Royce was far from being a talented striker, and he knew that to achieve success against Sakuraba, he would have to get him to the ground and keep him there.

Royce was the first to enter the ring, followed by the other fighting Gracies—even the senior Helio made it out for the fight. The crowd booed as Royce took his spot in the ring but quickly changed their mood when the lights dimmed for Sakuraba's entrance. Instead of their hero, the crowd saw three men in Mexican wrestling masks. And there was an extra surprise; before the real Sakuraba was introduced, Antonio Inoki made a special appearance in the ring to wish the fighters well before the start of the bout. Finally, when the announcer called Sakuraba's name, he peeled off his mask, much to the delight of the crowd.

At the ring of the bell, Gracie went straight at the Japanese fighter with a flurry of punches, but it was Sakuraba who shot for Royce's midsection and took him down to the mat. As the fight progressed, Sakuraba continued to put on a show for the crowd, at one point smirking to the crowd as he tried to put Royce's arm into a lock. Into the second round, Royce pushed with all his energy to finish the fight in style while Sakuraba stood back and waited for opportunities to arise.

Then came the controversial missed tap out. Backed into a corner, Royce held Sakuraba in a standing headlock, slowly cutting off his circulation. In the video replay, it was clear that Sakuraba could not escape the hold and was on the verge of passing out. He submitted by tapping on Gracie's leg. But the referee did not see the tap and the fight was allowed to continue. Saved by the missed call and the end of the round, the two fighters continued their epic battle.

The two fighters exchanged punches and kicks for over 90 minutes, with Sakuraba delivering the majority of painful blows. By the later stages of the match, Royce looked tired and defeated, hoping to hang on until the end. Countless punches landed directly to Royce's face, knocking him to the ground several times. As the fight wore on, the Gracie family in Royce's corner could see that he was on the verge of losing the fight and could not stand much more punishment from the Japanese fighter. In the pause between rounds, Royce admitted defeat and the white flag finally dropped in the ring. Sakuraba had won. The pride of the Gracie family had gone down in defeat, and Sakuraba became a legend.

With that victory, Pride was now firmly established as the globe's premiere fighting network, and Sakuraba was its main attraction. But the Gracie family had a reputation to uphold, and they were not about to let this cocky Japanese fighter soil the family legacy. For the next fight at Pride 10 on August 27, 2000, Renzo Gracie would step up and face the family nemesis.

Renzo was a different challenge for Sakuraba. While Royce posed the biggest technical challenge, Renzo was the more well-rounded fighter who could as easily surprise on the ground as he could standing up in a straight boxing match. By this time, the Gracie family had learned to respect the brash Japanese fighter, but their taste for revenge was even stronger now. "Kazushi Sakuraba was a stone in our shoes," said Renzo. "He was one of the most amazing fighters who came from Japan, and most amazing was his ability to play smart."

The fight turned out to be everything the fans had hoped for. From the opening round, both men went after each other, holding nothing back. They landed punches without impunity, kicks hit with a power that could chop down a tree, and yet the fighters continued after each other, one fighting for family honor, and the other, it seemed, for fun. Sakuraba tried everything in his arsenal to down Renzo early in the fight—flying kicks, two-handed over-the-head punches and his most famous cartwheel mounts.

Cartwheel mount: A fighter literally does a cartwheel over a downed opponent with the intention of gaining the advantage by passing his guard.

Despite the flash and attempts at finishing the fight with one swift knockout, the end came during one of the more innocent moments of the bout. Renzo had grabbed Sakuraba from behind while they were both standing, but this left his arm vulnerable, and Sakuraba took advantage. Yet again it was the Kimura hold that would take down another Gracie, but Renzo refused to tap out. The referee had to stop the fight when it became clear that Renzo's arm had been dislocated.

"To be honest, I enjoyed that moment. Because I was plenty conscious of what was going on and I didn't give up," said Renzo about the fight. "I saw the ligaments going and I heard them, one by one, giving way. And I embraced that as punishment for the mistake I had made. I really believed I could keep fighting, even without the arm." But he could not, and he accepted the loss to the better fighter.

After this event, the Japanese newspapers began to call Sakuraba the "Gracie Hunter." Pride fighting was at its peak popularity, with tens of thousands of fans attending the live events and millions of television viewers around the world. But the Sakuraba era in Pride was soon to come to a crushing end. It wasn't a Gracie that knocked Sakuraba off his throne but a Brazilian nonetheless: one Wanderlei Silva.

At Pride 13 on March 25, 2001, Silva knocked Sakuraba out cold with a devastating series of knee hits to the head in the first round. This was only Sakuraba's second defeat in mixed martial arts history, and despite the speed with which he was taken out, he wanted one more shot at Silva and redemption. But again Sakuraba was outmatched by the muscular Brazilian and was knocked out with a powerful punch to the jaw, effectively ending the Sakuraba era in Pride.

Interest in Pride continued through the beginning of the new millennium, but without a native Japanese star, it was evident that Pride was beginning to slip. That is not to say that the entertaining fights suddenly halted. Fighters such as Silva, Antonio Rodrigo Nogueira, Fedor Emelianenko, Chuck Liddell and Quinton "Rampage" Jackson kept the crowds coming back and the television audiences tuning in, but the lack of an entertaining Japanese star hurt the marketing value of the Pride brand. Takanori Gomi in 2005 and Kazuo Misaki in 2006 happened to win at Pride main events, but they could not sustain any success. Even with major Japanese stars, the end of Pride was just around the corner.

For several years, rumors had been circling that the Japanese mafia, the Yakuza, had become involved in the operation

SIDESHOW

In a strange attempt to market Pride around the world, Dream Stage Entertainment hinted that they had signed Mike Tyson to fight in their big 2007 New Year's Eve Show. The only catch was that Tyson would fight under the rules of boxing and not MMA. But because of Tyson's criminal record, he was not allowed to fight in Japan. A suitable alternate location could not be found, so the Tyson fight never materialized.

of Pride fights. The decreasing popularity of Pride, the absence of a marketable Japanese star and rumors of Yakuza involvement were too much for Pride's television broadcaster, Fuji TV, and in 2006, they cancelled their contract with Pride's parent company, Dream Stage Entertainment. Without the television audiences and the revenues the events brought in, Pride was doomed. One year later, in October 2007, Pride closed its Japanese offices, and most of Pride's top talent picked up and left for North America to fight in the UFC.

Rise of the New Gladiators

Bad men are full of repentance.

–Aristotle

It is better to be feared than loved, if you cannot be both.

–Niccolo Machiavelli

Everyone looks good punching bricks.

–Art Davie

The Origins of the Octagon and Beyond

Rorion Gracie had a clear purpose: to spread the word of his family's brand of martial arts to the world and prove it superior to all other challengers. He thought he could sell this idea to fight fans in North America. The only problem in the beginning was that no one seemed interested.

After moving to the U.S. in 1978 and struggling to establish himself for over 10 years, Rorion Gracie had some luck landing a few acting roles on the Hollywood movie lots as an extra or as a stuntman, but this was not his idea of success. By the late 1980s, he changed direction and started his own martial arts academy and brought his brothers to the U.S., but again, he wanted more—he wanted it all.

In 1989, things started to come together for the Gracie family. Writer Pat Jordan stumbled upon Gracie jiujitsu and Rorion Gracie, and he thought that Rorion and his brand of fighting would make a great article for the testosterone readers of *Playboy* magazine.

In the September 1989 issue, the magazine ran a feature titled "Bad" that detailed the Gracie family story and the effectiveness of their Brazilian jiujitsu. It began: "Rorion Gracie is willing to fight to the death to prove he's the toughest man in the west." The article described Rorion as "dark and handsome like Tom Selleck, with wavy black hair, a trim mustache and a charming, self-deprecating smile" but then quickly shifted focus to one of his fights with a tough, imposing kickboxer whom Rorion defeated in less than three minutes via a choke out. But the most important part of the story stated that Rorion made a public offer to fight anyone in the United States for a winner-take-all prize of $100,000.

So far he has had no takers—for one simple reason. Rorion's fights are fights to the finish with no rules. His fights are merely street brawls in a ring bounded by ropes. Kicking, punching, head butting, elbow and knee hits are all fair play in a Gracie fight. Only the accouterments of a street brawl—broken bottles, ash cans, bricks—are missing. The only purpose the referee serves in a Gracie fight is to acknowledge his opponent's surrender when he taps the mat with his hand or passes out from a choke hold.

With the raw violence and bravado dripping off the pages of the magazine, it wasn't long before someone realized the potential in Rorion Gracie, and that person was the opportunist/advertising executive Art Davie. Together, Rorion and Davie produced a series of tapes marketing the Gracie brand of fighting, which was a minor success but really took both men nowhere. To open up the world to Gracie jiujitsu, the two men focused on that one paragraph in the *Playboy* article that detailed Rorion's plans to take on any challengers. Davie and Rorion brought in friend and movie director John Milius (*Conan, Red Dawn*) to brainstorm ideas on how to market the Gracie Challenge concept. Davie stated:

> *Milius, Gracie, and I were sitting around talking one night and we began a conversation, like guys used to have in Vietnam about if Sugar Ray Robinson were alive and fought Bruce Lee, who would win. People always have those "what if?" conversations in the martial arts. Out of it came a desire to do this event.*

From there, Davie and Rorion formed a company called WOW (War of the Worlds), and they set up several meetings with television executives to try to sell them on their idea. They were flatly turned down. The excuses given included "It's too violent," "There is no market for it," "The world already has boxing and wrestling; it will never survive." HBO and Showtime rejected the idea once they heard the pitch, as did pay-per-view companies that regularly broadcast pornography. When all looked hopeless, Davie and Rorion finally got a bite from the Semaphore Entertainment Group.

The head of the group, Bob Meyrowitz, had never heard of a mixed martial arts fight and was not interested in promoting a new sport. However, Meyrowitz was intrigued by the violence of the proposed competition and the amount of people who would want to see it. What sold the company was a grainy tape of Rickson Gracie on a beach in Brazil dealing out fistfuls of justice to a man who had been insulting the Gracie name. The only problem was, basically, taking a brutal street fight and selling it to the public. But the potential for success was there, and now all Semaphore had to do was to figure out how to package it all.

The initial idea was to make the event a monthly battle of martial arts warriors, but Rorion and the company finally settled on a one-night tournament to crown a champion. Some executives at Semaphore thought that a standard boxing ring would be sufficient to hold the spectacle, but Rorion was concerned that the fighters could be thrown out of the ring and severely injured. When the ancient Greeks held their Pankration fights, it had been suggested that they used octagon-shaped arenas, so this was the type of arena settled on for Rorion's War of the Worlds battle.

The octagon would give television viewers a perfect unobstructed view of the action and provide a safe way to contain the fighters. The problem now was the name of the event because "War of the Worlds" invoked an image of aliens more than martial arts. The Semaphore vice president of marketing came up with the name "Ultimate

Fighting Championship," and suddenly a new phenomenon was born. Once these details were ironed out, all that remained was to find the fighters and a place to hold the ultimate spectacle.

At 41 years of age, Rorion was too old to fight anymore, so he turned to his brother Royce to represent the family in the first UFC. The reason he chose Royce was not obvious, as his brother Rickson had a much larger physique and a solid history as a street brawler. But Rorion wanted Royce because he afforded the opportunity to display the power of Gracie jiujitsu. To have a skinny fighter take down and make a man much larger than himself cry out in pain would be the perfect way to show the world that Gracie jiujitsu could beat all others.

To enhance the mixed martial arts program, organizers added kickboxers Kevin Rosier, an over-the-hill fighter with an enormous beer gut; Pat Smith, a local fighter of some acclaim; and Zane Frazier. Frazier had achieved a level of fame for beating up Frank Dux, the karate fighter who served as the inspiration for Jean-Claude Van Damme's *Bloodsport*.

They also found vicious street fighter Gerard Gordeau. A savate and karate expert, Gordeau was employed as a bouncer and a bodyguard for pornography film producers in Europe and was

"FRENCH FU"

Also known as French kick-boxing, *savate* is the French word for "old boot," a type of heavy footwear worn during the 19th century in France. Savate started out as a mix of French street-fighting techniques and was later formalized into its own martial art.

known to have sent a few men to hospital with life-threatening injuries.

Boxer Art Jimmerson also joined the motley crew of fighters. The addition of a pure boxer was specifically requested by Rorion. The Gracie family had long wanted to put their skills up against a talented boxer, with Helio Gracie going as far as to challenge the great heavyweight Joe Louis while Rickson had put in his request to fight Mike Tyson, but neither fight ever materialized. Boxing was well known to the public as the dominant fighting sport, and the Gracies wanted nothing more than to show the world how weak the "sweet science" actually was.

The final fighter was a 400-pound sumo wrestler named Teila Tuli, who struck an imposing image but seemed to have been added to the group for the sheer spectacle. Regardless, Tuli was more than serious about his chances in the tournament, saying, "I came here to fight. I'll fight anyone who wants to fight."

The first UFC would also need a grand stage on which to show its unique product. Organizers ended up settling on the McNichols Sports Arena in Denver, Colorado, with a seating capacity of around 16,000. With the lineup in order, the first Ultimate Fighting Championship looked very similar to the Street Fighter video game series of 1988, and the promoters were hoping to attract many of those fans. The sumo wrestler, the exotic Brazilian, the kickboxer—the list of fighters seemed to make the event more of a sideshow than a reputable martial arts tournament. What it needed to achieve a base level of credibility was a world-class fighter who would silence the detractors, and that person was Ken Shamrock.

Ken Shamrock

Born on February 11, 1964, in Macon, Georgia, Kenneth Wayne Kilpatrick's life was not kind from the beginning. Although his mother did everything she could to keep a roof over her sons' heads and keep them fed, life was never easy being raised by a single mother in poor rural Georgia. Without a father figure in his life, young Ken was left by his overworked mother to wander the streets of his neighborhood with his brothers and his friends, getting into all kinds of trouble. He first ran away from home when he was 10 years old, spending his time hiding out in an abandoned car with other kids on the run. The police eventually found him when a fellow runaway sent him to the hospital with a stab wound after the pair had gotten into an argument. Even with such a scare, Ken did not change his ways and continued to be a source of stress for his mother and the authorities.

Unable to take care of her son, Ken's mother was forced to place him in a group home for delinquent boys. However, over the next few years, he was thrown out of several homes and even served time in a prison for juveniles. Entering into his teens and with no signs of a change of attitude, as a last resort he was shipped off to California to live in another group home.

But this home was different. The Shamrock Ranch, run by Bob Shamrock, had a long and well-respected history of working with and rehabilitating troubled kids. Unlike the way other group homes were managed, Bob Shamrock had a unique method of dealing with conflicts that arose in the home. Instead of having the boys talk things out all the time, and if both sides were willing, he tossed them boxing gloves and allowed them to take out their frustrations on each other in the yard. It didn't take long for Ken to become undisputed champion of the home. He was so happy in his new home that he adopted

Bob Shamrock as his surrogate father, even going as far as changing his last name from Kilpatrick to Shamrock. Outside of these group-home fights, Ken could not help but get into a few fights out on the town, and in a short time he earned himself a dubious reputation.

"He'd get into a fight and just knock the guy out," recalled Bob Shamrock. "He hit them once and they were down. He never picked fights, but he never backed away from them."

However, if Ken did not get any direction soon, he would most certainly end up behind bars. Recognizing Ken's innate athletic talents, Bob started him on a weight-training program and then enrolled him in wrestling and football. Football was a fun distraction, but Ken wasn't much of a team player, preferring to prove his skills in a wrestling or boxing ring rather than on a football field.

At the age of 19, Ken came across the Toughman competition and thought it would be fun to enter and test out his skills. The fights were organized similar to a playoff format, where, if you won your first fight, you progressed into the next round until someone was declared champion. For Ken Shamrock's first official fight inside a ring, he was put up against a fighter who outweighed him by 60 pounds, but that did not stop the 195-pound teenager from knocking his opponent out with a powerful body shot. Shamrock then knocked out the second challenger, as well as several of his teeth. This win moved Shamrock into the final round for the championship, but his opponent refused to get into the ring, faking an injury and surrendering the title rather than risk fighting Shamrock.

Shamrock bounced around through a few odd jobs, working as a bouncer, even fighting in back alleys for money, but each job proved to be a dead end. Then one day, Bob suggested to Ken that he go into professional wrestling. They traveled to North Carolina to enroll Ken in a well-known wrestling school. In a matter of months, Ken became involved in the local wrestling circuit in North Carolina but found the payoffs not worth the effort he had to put in. Then came the opportunity that would change his life.

MACHISMO

Have you ever imagined how you would do if you were placed in a ring and given boxing gloves? Well, in 1979, an ambitious boxing promoter named Art Dore started the Toughman competition to give a novice amateur fighter the chance to prove his or her worth inside a state-sanctioned fight. Even in states that did not sanction these fights, they often were held illegally.

A friend showed him a tape of the Universal Wrestling Federation (UWF) in Japan, and Ken instantly knew what he wanted to do. In North America, wrestling had become more theater than sport, but in Japan, although the fights were still fixed, the promoters tried to keep the sport grounded in technique. It wasn't long after seeing the tape that Ken boarded a plane and headed straight for Japan.

While he was in the United States, Ken Shamrock had been one of the best wrestlers and fighters, but in Japan, he was quickly taught a lesson in humility. During practice sessions with UWF stars Minoru Suzuki and Akira Maeda, the veteran submission wrestlers regularly beat Shamrock, an experience he fully embraced:

> I've always been able to pretty much handle myself in any situation. But when I went to Japan, the technique there was so much better that I was getting heal-hooked, arm barred, and choked. I was like, "Oh my God, this stuff is great."

Although it took him several years to master, Shamrock had found the technique that made him into a complete fighter. He absorbed as much technique as he could from his Japanese wrestling mentors while he wrestled for the UWF. The Japanese fighters were still the stars of the shows, but Shamrock began to form a loyal following of his own. Things were going well, but then the UWF fell apart, with several of the wrestlers going their separate ways to form new wrestling organizations.

Shamrock followed fellow wrestlers Masakatsu Funaki and Minoru Suzuki into their new wrestling group called Pancrase, which was still based around wrestling techniques but would partially remove the theatrics of the old wrestling style. Once unleashed from the bonds of the fixed fight, Shamrock proved to be a difficult opponent to defeat. He was armed with deadly boxing power, a solid wrestling foundation and sound grappling techniques.

Feeling confident in his future in the developing sport of mixed martial arts fighting, Shamrock returned to the United States and founded the now famous Lion's Den training facility, where many future stars of the UFC would get their start. At first, Shamrock opened it to be a training point for American fighters to go to Japan to fight in Pancrase, but in 1993 while flipping through an issue of *Black Belt* magazine, he came across an advertisement searching for martial arts experts to compete in a bare-knuckle fighting event called the Ultimate Fighting Championship.

The Burp Heard Around the World

With all the eight fighters now on board for the first Ultimate Fighting Championship, the fans packed into McNichols Sports Arena, ready to watch the event take the world by storm. Eager fight fans at home around the world turned on their television sets and readied themselves for what was being marketed as "No rules fighting."

Rather than beginning with energy and hype, UFC 1 began with a burp, literally. Semaphore had hired professional full-contact karate champion Bill "Superfoot" Wallace and given him the important job of introducing this new sport to the world, but as he fumbled through his opening lines, he belched. "Hi, I'm Bill Wallace and welcome to Manic...burp...excuse me—to McNichols Arena in fabulous Denver, Colorado."

Not only did Wallace screw up by belching on live television, but he also named the tournament incorrectly, calling it the "Ultimate Fighting Challenge" instead of "Championship." Organizers had hoped that pulling in a recognizable name like Bill Wallace would provide the UFC with a certain level of credibility, but that flew out the window within the first few seconds of the broadcast.

Wallace might not have been the greatest choice, but adding former NFL football player and all-around tough guy Jim Brown provided the broadcast with a little humor amid the seriousness. As well as the initial bump, or burp, more serious worries were going on behind the scenes. Because MMA was a new sport to television, no one in the broadcasting booth knew how long the fights would last. The Gracies had already proven that they could take opponents out in minutes, and in some cases, mere seconds. The broadcasters were faced with the real possibility of having nothing to show the millions of people at home watching on pay-per-view after 30 minutes, given that there were only eight fighters in total. In a boxing match, fans are pretty much guaranteed fights that last more than five rounds, at three minutes per round, but for the inaugural UFC, broadcasters were flying blind and praying they wouldn't crash.

UFC 1 Quarter Finals

Teila Tuli (6', 2"; 440 lbs.)
vs.
Gerard Gordeau (6', 5"; 224 lbs.)

It would be a true battle of mixed martial arts. Teila Tuli (born Taylor Wiley) was recruited into the world of sumo in the mid-1980s and left his Hawaiian home to live and train in Japan. He was one of the largest sumo wrestlers in

Japan and learned to use his size to dominate opponents. In a short span of time, he became the first foreign-born wrestler to win the championship in his division and even was honored with becoming the mentor of another American sumo-wrestling hopeful, future Yokosuka champion Akebono.

Tuli wrestled in Japan from 1987 to 1989 and retired from the sport when it was clear he could not reach the higher divisions because of too many losses. He returned to the United States, where learned of the UFC and decided to give it a try. Many were surprised to see a trained sumo wrestler in the UFC 1 competition, given that the discipline is more sport than martial art, but Tuli obviously felt he could compete in the ring against other opponents.

THESPIAN

A man of many talents, Tuli appeared in the 2007 Hollywood comedy *Forgetting Sarah Marshall*, playing the role of the loveable hotel worker who befriends the main character. Tuli currently has a recurring role on the CBS television series *Hawaii Five-O*.

Gerard Gordeau was no stranger to the world of fighting. From 1978 to 1985, he had dominated the Dutch Karate Championship, fought in several no-holds-barred fights in the Netherlands and, after his brief stint with the UFC, he traveled to Japan where he fought under the Rings network. Naturally, because of his experience, Gordeau was given the advantage over Tuli, but in an open, no-rules fight, predicting the outcome was impossible.

One of the most interesting aspects of the early UFC fights was the outfits the fighters wore. Gordeau showed up in a pair of traditional gi pants used in judo and karate, while Tuli wore a traditional Samoan lava-lava (basically a skirt decorated with various patterns).

There was a definite sense of excitement in the air as the two fighters took to their corners and were introduced to the audience. The fight began with Tuli charging toward Gordeau and giving him an aggressive push using a series of open-hand sumo slaps (for those who have played the video game Street Fighter, it would be hard not to think of the character E. Honda, who performed a similar move in the game). It's difficult to figure out what Tuli hoped to achieve with this maneuver, but it failed miserably when Gordeau simply tossed him aside. With Tuli in a vulnerable spot on his knees, Gordeau finished him off with one roundhouse kick to the face followed by a right hook. Video replay shows one of Tuli's teeth flying out of the octagon as he absorbed the kick. Gordeau was left with a souvenir from the kick—two of Tuli's teeth embedded in his foot. UFC doctors decided to leave the teeth in because they did not want to leave Gordeau with an open wound for the rest of the tournament.

After just 26 seconds, the fight was officially stopped because of a cut above Tuli's eye, but it was evident that even if he could have continued, Tuli wanted nothing more to do with the UFC. Tuli might have gotten out of that fight in better shape than Gordeau though, because on top of having two of Tuli's teeth in his foot, Gordeau had broken his hand when he delivered that right punch to the sumo's fat head.

Kevin Rosier (6', 4"; 265 lbs.)
vs.
Zane Frazier (6', 6"; 230 lbs.)

If they had been worried earlier about the lengths of the fights, the producer and directors of the first UFC were now panicking after the first fight ended in 26 seconds.

"There are 11 cameras and you're watching everything," Semaphore programmer Campbell McClaren is quoted as saying in the book *Total MMA* by Jonathan Snowden.

We're in that truck for the first fight between Teila Tuli and Gerard Gordeau and it lasted, like, four seconds or something. And we're thinking, "We've got 11 fights, we've got a three-hour block, but this might be a four-minute show." We had no idea even how long the fights were going to last.

The next fight of the evening was between overweight Kevin Rossier (the former North American kickboxing champion) and Kempo karate practitioner Zane Frazier. It was a battle of the super heavyweights.

Rosier was the first to start throwing punches while chasing Frazier around the octagon. After this strange opening, both fighters finally squared off against each other, with Rosier landing the first punch and sending Frazier to the ground. The punch seemed to anger Frazier, who got up and slammed Rosier into the octagon cage and then grabbed him by his hair and kneed him in the groin and stomach. Rosier managed to get off the cage and back out into the open. But at this point, it was obvious to the crowd that both big men had used all their energy in the opening minutes of the bout, with Frazier looking the worst of the two. Unable to keep his hands up to protect himself, Frazier took a powerful right hook to the face that sent him crashing to the ground. Rosier followed that up with a series of punches and stomps to the back of Frazier's head until his corner threw in the towel.

Although the crowd loved that the fight had lasted longer than a few seconds, it was clear that both fighters were out of shape and not that good. The two fighters were practitioners of respected martial arts, but when placed in a real situation, they resorted to cheap street-fighting tactics. Nevertheless, Rosier advanced to the next round.

Royce Gracie (6', 1"; 180 lbs.)
vs.
Art Jimmerson (6', 1"; 196 lbs.)

The next fight introduced the world to Royce Gracie. He certainly did not strike an imposing figure, wearing his jiujitsu gi and weighing a scrawny 180 pounds. Most people took one look at the Brazilian and thought that boxer Art Jimmerson would destroy him with one punch.

Jimmerson was a career pro boxer who entered the UFC simply for the money to help in the purchase of a new house. He figured that he could walk into an arena with other martial artists, and, with a few fancy moves, lay them out flat with a right-hand punch. After all, he had spent his life training in the ring and knew how to take a hit.

While watching the first two fights, Jimmerson felt good about his chances in the octagon, but when he saw Ken Shamrock working out with a partner, he suddenly felt out of place.

Future UFC referee "Big" John McCarthy was there as Gracie's training partner and remembered Jimmerson's attitude before the fight:

> *The one thing I remember today as clearly as that day back on November 12, 1993, was Art Jimmerson having a panicked look on his face when he said, "Oh, my god, he is going to break my arms and legs, isn't he?"*

Even though Jimmerson looked ridiculous walking into the octagon wearing one boxing glove, the crowd cheered for the boxer whom they assumed would most certainly knock the head off the skinny Brazilian. However, as soon as the fight began, it had already ended. Within seconds, Gracie had the mount position and had not yet put Jimmerson into a submission hold when Jimmerson feverishly began to tap out.

The crowd was incensed at the outcome of the fight and rained down a violent chorus of boos on the octagon. This was the first time the world was seeing Gracie jiujitsu, and it was only natural to react in such a way when coming to see a fight marketed as no rules, no holds barred. The fans had paid money to see a good fight, but instead, the audience at home and in the arena would get more incensed in the next fight.

Mount position is the dominant ground-fighting position in which the aggressor straddles his opponent's abdomen. This position allows the aggressor almost full control of a fight and forces his opponent to go on the defensive.

Ken Shamrock (6', 220 lbs.)
vs.
Patrick Smith (6', 2"; 217 lbs.)

When the hulking frame of Ken Shamrock walked into the arena, the crowd expected a bloody fight. He had the look of someone ready to explode and hurt anyone who got in his way. But Patrick Smith was no pushover himself, having studied taekwondo, hapkido, karate and tang soo so, all different types of martial arts. He also had a terrifying record in bare-knuckle fights of 250 wins and zero losses.

When the bell rang, the two fighters squared off, and Smith made the first move with a hard front kick to Shamrock's midsection. The kick connected but glanced off to the side, allowing Shamrock to grab Smith and take him to the ground in the mount position. Smith attempted to break Shamrock's hold with a series of vicious heel strikes to his kidneys. Shamrock, though, held firm and was able to open up Smith's guard with a few punches to the ribs. Spotting his opening, Shamrock fell back and put Smith into a leg lock. Smith tried to break free, but his opponent gripped harder on the heel hook, forcing Smith to tap out.

In just under two minutes, the fight had ended, and again the crowd was not happy about the

Heel hook: The fighter gets hold of his opponent's leg and then locks it between his body and his arm. He then applies pressure to the ankle and twists his body, thereby hyperextending the ankle.

outcome. "They were mad. No one understood what submission was," said Shamrock in a later interview. "Even the announcer was like, 'He got him in some foot lock or something.'"

The crowd might not have enjoyed the spectacle, but it set the stage for the next round in which Shamrock would face off against Royce Gracie in one of the sport's most iconic moments.

UFC 1 Semifinals

Gerard Gordeau vs. Kevin Rosier

The second round opened up with two tired and injured fighters. Gerard Gordeau still had two of Teila Tuli's teeth embedded in his foot and was also nursing a broken right hand, while Kevin Rosier looked tired and ready to call it quits. When the bell rang, Rosier tried to set the tone of the fight by attacking Gordeau with a few test jabs. Gordeau baited him into thinking he was backing off, but once Rosier was close, Gordeau hacked at his legs to set up a right punch to Rosier's jaw that knocked him to the ground. Rosier tried to get up, but Gordeau kept throwing punches and elbows along with a few flying heel stomps for good measure. Before Rosier could make it back to his feet, the referee called an end to the fight. Gordeau advanced to the finals on his victory and waited for the winner of the Gracie-Shamrock fight.

Royce Gracie vs. Ken Shamrock

Looking at the fighters ahead of him, Shamrock felt confident in his ability to win the entire tournament, having, in his mind, already beaten the toughest fighter of the competition. After all, Shamrock had been fighting his whole life and had beaten the best fighters in Japan. He had seen Gracie up against Jimmerson and did not think he had much to worry about. Nobody knew it at the time, but this was the beginning of one of the most entertaining and intense rivalries in mixed martial arts history.

"When I went in there, I didn't know who Royce Gracie was," said Shamrock. "When he came out and I saw him with a gi, I said, 'Karate guy. I'll take him no problem.' I saw all these boxers and said, 'Everybody's a stand-up. I'll smoke these guys.'"

The fight started off with Royce going immediately for the take down, but Shamrock was no rookie in the submission world and sprawled his legs to defend against giving Gracie the mount. It appeared to most people in the arena and to those watching at home on television that Shamrock had the advantage, but little did they know that Gracie was as effective technically from the guard as from the mount position.

From that point, it became a wrestling match,

HALF GUARD/HALF MOUNT

A position in which the fight -er on the bottom is able to trap one of his opponent's legs, thus preventing him from gaining the full mount position.

with each fighter working for the most advantageous position. Shamrock made the first attempt at breaking the stalemate by trying to get to his feet. Then Gracie went into the half guard position. When Shamrock tried to roll out by moving to his belly, it left Gracie the opportunity to choke him out. The fight ended after 57 seconds, with Shamrock tapping out. The referee had not seen the tap out, but Shamrock was an honest fighter and admitted defeat. Gracie had humbled Shamrock in the octagon, but the two fighters would meet again soon enough.

UFC 1 Final

During the last semifinal, Gerard Gordeau sat in the dressing room with his hands plunged deep in ice buckets. His right hand from the fight with Tuli had swollen to twice its size, and now is left hand was broken and began to swell after his tilt with Rosier. But despite the severity of his injuries, Gordeau said that he would continue the fight. He simply wrapped up his hands and walked out into the octagon for the final fight. He was not about to let something as trivial as two broken hands stop him. Gracie entered the fight having barely broken a sweat.

Rear naked choke: One fighter gains control of his opponent's back, slips an arm around his neck and chokes him until he either taps out or passes out. Similar to the guillotine choke (see page 203).

When the bell rang to start the fight, Gracie immediately shot inside for a leg takedown, but Gordeau held on, and both fighters went crashing into the cage. However, with his injuries, Gordeau could not hold on for long and was taken to the ground. Organizers of the fight were aware of Gordeau's history of violence and tendency to use any means necessary to win, and now, put in a position to lose the fight, Gordeau went back to his old tricks. With Gracie dominating the fight from the mount position, head in close to his opponent's chest, Gordeau took the opportunity to bite Gracie's ear "a la Mike Tyson." Fortunately, Gracie did not lose any part of his ear. This gutless move angered Gracie, and he instantly slipped out of the mount, turned Gordeau onto his stomach and choked him out. Gordeau frantically tapped out, but Gracie held on a little longer just to teach him a lesson.

After the Fight

With that UFC 1 victory, Royce Gracie became $50,000 richer and was recorded as the first official champion of the Ultimate Fighting Championship. While some of the fans walked out of the arena confused over what they had seen, the buzz surrounding the event was unlike any the prize-fighting world had ever witnessed. Despite the problems, the burps and the less-than-one-minute bouts, the UFC had struck a nerve with fans. They might have been unhappy at first, but they couldn't help but be curious at how a skinny Brazilian could win a fight so easily against a fighter twice his size.

Other fighting competitions would try to establish themselves in the same fashion as the UFC, but they were missing the magic that happened that night in Denver. The world had long debated the question of whether a wrestler could beat a boxer, and the UFC was the first to give a definitive answer. Japan's Pancrase, Rings and Pride had all tried to achieve the same level of success prior to UFC 1, and despite being very popular in Japan, ultimate fighting never really caught on in the rest of the world.

A major reason for the success of the UFC was its often shameless promotion of the violent aspect of the sport. Tag lines from the press, such as "Two Men Enter, One Man Leaves" and "Banned in 49 States," helped to garner attention for the sport, and in turn, the media became the biggest advertisers for the UFC. But the best advertisers were the young men across North America who told their friends about this incredible event they had seen—and this was all done by word of mouth, as the age of the Internet had only just begun.

In a matter of a few short months, young men were practicing the moves they saw in UFC 1 in their basements with their friends and their little brothers. They had grown up believing what they had seen in the movies—that Bruce Lee could defeat anyone with his powerful kung fu, and that Chuck Norris could knock out a guy with one kick (ok, so maybe Chuck Norris could actually do this). But then Royce Gracie came along, and he proved that while the other martial arts may be flashy, they didn't work in real life.

This realization, of course, upset the established martial arts world, as the UFC was costing them hard cash. Even the announcer of UFC 1, Bill Wallace, wrote a scathing letter to *Black Belt* magazine putting down submission fighting. But potential students no longer wanted to learn karate or kung fu; instead, they took Brazilian jiujitsu classes. Although there were a few detractors of the sport, there was an overwhelmingly positive response from the fans, who craved another UFC event.

The Second UFC

While opinions on the Ultimate Fighting brand continued to rage, event organizers were busy planning its second installment. Given the reaction of fans and fighters after the first event, some changes to the rules were deemed in order. Although it was marketed as no-rules fighting, the first UFC still had regulations that fighters had to follow.

In the first event, fighters were barred from striking the groin area, but many competitors skilled in karate complained that the rule took away a technique they had trained for. Event organizers also lowered the number of rounds because, in the first UFC, not one fighter made it past the first round.

UFC 2 would also be where the legendary referee "Big" John McCarthy would make his first appearance. A police officer at the time, McCarthy was the perfect man for the job; he made decisive calls, and his 250-pound physique could handle the fighters in the ring when things became heated. McCarthy would become as famous as many of the fighters, with his well-known line, "You ready? You ready? Let's get it on!"

The second UFC was again held in Denver on March 14, 1994, and 2000 fans attended the live broadcast while over 300,000 people paid to have the fight beamed directly into their homes or local bars. Another difference from the original event was that this time around, organizers did not have any trouble finding a better class of fighters. Applications to participate in the second UFC poured in from all corners of the world: Spain, France, Japan, Brazil and the Netherlands. However, one important fighter was missing from the group; Ken Shamrock was forced to sit out from a rematch with Royce Gracie because of a broken arm suffered in a training accident. So 16 fighters started the event, and only one would win the $60,000 purse.

Although the fighters were better and a few of them had training in some submission techniques, Royce Gracie again dominated the field and easily won the final over returning fighter Patrick Smith, via submission, of course. The fight was a success, but overall, the event itself lacked the flair and theater that would propel the sport to new audiences. UFC 3 would not make that mistake.

UFC 3

Held in Charlotte, North Carolina, UFC 3 was billed as the rematch of Royce Gracie versus Ken Shamrock. The two fighters appeared on the poster promoting the event that was to take place on September 9, 1994. However, the epic rematch was not a sure thing because the fight lineup was selected by a draw of numbered ping-pong balls. The two fighters ended up on opposite sides of the bracket, with the only possible place for either of them to meet being in the finals.

Besides Gracie and Shamrock, this third UFC had a lineup of exciting fighters for the audience. It saw the return of another sumo wrestler, this time 6-foot-8, 600-pound giant Emmanuel Yarborough, and the introduction to the fighting world of Kimo Leopoldo, a taekwondo fighter. This was the kind of man you would not want to meet in a dark alley. He had the look of a killer, with religious symbols tattooed over most of his body and a muscular frame that put the fear of

God into his opponents. He was just the fighter the UFC wanted to promote their event.

The first fight of the night was Keith Hackney versus Emmanuel Yarborough. It was almost comical to see the two fighters in the ring, as Yarborough clearly had a significant height and weight advantage over the 5-foot-11, 200-pound Hackney. Yet again, David would defeat Goliath.

Ken Shamrock easily defeated his opponent, Christophe Leininger, and then anxiously waited on the sidelines for the outcome of the Gracie versus Kimo bout, hoping to have his chance at revenge.

The Gracie fight was quite the spectacle. The muscle-bound Kimo started the bout by a cinematic emergence into the arena through a veil of smoke, carrying a giant wooden cross on his back. Gracie, as usual, arrived with his entire family behind him as support. The crowd was buzzing—it appeared to most that Gracie might have finally met his match in Kimo, and for the first few moments of the battle, it seemed that Gracie might be in trouble for the first time in the UFC's early history.

Kimo was able to keep Gracie from taking him to the ground, where Gracie was his most dangerous, and as a result, Gracie took a few good punches for his failure. But eventually the two men fell to the ground, and again Kimo used his strength to stay one step ahead. Gracie kept Kimo from locking him in a submission move, but for the first time since UFC began, he seemed to be struggling. Although they had only been battling for about four minutes, Gracie had expended nearly all his energy in keeping Kimo from smashing him into a bloody pulp, and he desperately needed a way out of the fight. The fight began to turn in Gracie's favor only when he grabbed a fistful of Kimo's hair (not against the rules at the time) and gained control of his opponent. He then finished Kimo off with an arm bar, but he had to be dragged to the dressing room by his family members because he had used so much energy in trying to hold on to Kimo.

In the semifinals, Shamrock easily submitted Felix Lee Mitchell, but in the process injured his leg and was out of the tournament, losing out on his chance to battle Gracie. That didn't really matter because Gracie could not continue either. He was still feeling the effects of his battle with Kimo, thereby conceding his semifinal match against Canadian fighter Harold Howard. As Shamrock could not compete in the final, alternate Steve Jennum was brought in to fight Howard, and Jennum ended up winning the tournament. The Gracie-Shamrock saga would have to wait.

The Fight Against Fighting

---

*Far from being legitimate sports events, ulti-
mate fighting contests are little more than
human cockfights where human gladiators battle bare-knuckled until one gives up, passes out,
or the carnage is stopped by a doctor or referee.*

–Lonnie Brostow, president of the
American Medical Association

*You know, I just went from the barstool to
the Octagon.*

–Tank Abbott

The Wrong Kind of Attention

In the two short years since it first appeared in
1993, the Ultimate Fighting Championship
had become an underground phenomenon.

Across North America, young men passed around tapes of the events, practiced the moves in their basements and argued over which fighter was the best. And while a younger generation fell in love with the spectacle, their parents had a different view of what the UFC was trying to accomplish.

The fifth installment of the Ultimate Fighting franchise, given the strange headline of "The Return of the Beast," was the event everyone was waiting for and would get people talking. Prior to the event that was to be held in Charlotte, North Carolina, on April 7, 1995, a rematch between Royce Gracie and Ken Shamrock was booked in a new event called the Superfight. Held outside the regular tournament, the Superfight between the two most popular fighters in the UFC's brief history would finally seek to answer the question of who was the greatest fighter.

Apart from the Gracie-Shamrock Superfight, UFC 5 held a great lineup of fighters who were guaranteed to put on a good show. Dan Severn, a trained wrestler, had appeared in UFC 4 and quickly earned himself a spot in the hearts of MMA fans after making it into the finals, only to lose against Royce Gracie.

No one knew what to make of Severn when he first stepped into the octagon for his

UFC 4 quarterfinal match against muay thai fighter Anthony Macias. After all, Severn had trained his entire life as a classic Greco-Roman wrestler. His brand of fighting was about technique, strength and intelligence. Depending on who you were fighting, in the octagon you could end up in a bloody fistfight or get your head stomped on. But the fears were quickly put aside when Severn grabbed his first challenger by the waist and launched him into the air with a straight back suplex, twice. This is something the UFC had never experienced, and fans loved it. Severn made it through to the finals on his strength and wrestling skills but ultimately lost the title when Royce Gracie put him in a triangle choke after nearly 16 minutes.

BACK SUPLEX

The fighter stands behind his opponent then simply lifts him by the torso and slams him on his back and sometimes even his head. It is a complex and dangerous move because it can lead to serious neck injury or even paralysis.

That loss would only serve to motivate Severn more, and he returned to UFC 5 having trained in submission techniques and ready for anything the other fighters could dish out. In his first UFC,

Severn had looked timid and unsure about how far he could take the fights, but for his return, he was a man prepared to make his mark and show no mercy.

In UFC 5, Dan Severn made it easily out of the quarterfinals and advanced to face the tournament's first Russian entry, Oleg Taktarov. A former soldier and KGB defense instructor, Taktarov was a new breed of UFC fighter, one who had actually put his training to use in the real world. Rorion Gracie had originally rejected the idea of Taktarov fighting in the UFC because the Russian had a high degree of real-world training and might go too far in the octagon. But having viewed a tape of his grappling skills, Art Davie overruled Gracie's decision and pushed Taktarov through. The decision would be both a blessing and a curse.

Severn and Taktarov struck imposing figures when standing in the octagon. Both were built like tanks and had the ferocity to back up their skills. Severn's first move was to try for a takedown the moment that referee John McCarthy screamed, "Let's get it on!" Severn succeeded and followed up with a violent flurry of punches, but nothing seemed to connect or even faze the cold calmness of the Russian. Severn ended up in the half guard, and the two fighters scurried about on the mat for a few minutes.

Severn did everything he could to try to pummel Taktarov's face into the ground, but the Russian looked completely calm despite eating a few punches. Taktarov then rolled in the half guard to try for an arm bar but couldn't fully lock it in before Severn hit him in the head with a few power knees that caused ugly cuts on Taktarov's forehead. Despite his inability to see through the cascade of blood pouring down his face and the continued assault of knees and punches from above, Taktarov held onto Severn's arm and was close to finishing off the maneuver when McCarthy stepped in to stop the fight.

Taktarov's face looked like it had been through a meat grinder, and his blood was smeared across the mat of the octagon, but despite this, Taktarov protested the stoppage. The protest fell on the deaf ears of those who could see what he looked like. While many fans loved the reality of the fight, it would be that image of blood and gore that many people outside the MMA world would use as a jumping point in the push to have ultimate fighting banned completely.

With Taktarov's bloodstain still visible on the octagon mat, Gracie and Shamrock entered the ring to do battle in the UFC's first Superfight.

The hype for the fight was the greatest in UFC history, but the actual bout turned out to be a huge disappointment for the fans. After the Severn-Taktarov blood match, the crowd wanted another violent fight, and given the way the fight had been promoted, it was almost expected. But fans got nothing of the kind; instead, the crowd and everyone watching the match at home were treated to a 36-minute grappling bout that saw little in the way of action and ended up with the referee calling the fight a draw.

When the two men were pulled from their loving embrace on the mat, the crowd immediately unleashed a chorus of boos down on the two once-beloved fighters. It was a fight to forget, and everyone did. Dan Severn went on to win the championship, but when it was over, most people would only talk about the violence and the sight of Taktarov covered in his own blood.

The Politicians and the Politics

Even in places where the UFC was legally allowed to hold events, there was always someone trying to shut them down. At UFC 2 in Denver in 1994, the mayor tried hard to stop it from happening and threatened to send in the police during the event. To be honest, the UFC was an easy target for any politician looking for an issue to stir up their constituents when election time loomed. The nature of the spectacle that was UFC in the early 1990s did not help its cause, either. Up against other prizefighting ventures, such as boxing, mixed martial arts looked downright brutal. It allowed hair pulling, punches to the groin and dangerous strikes that could lead to a fighter's death. Promoting the fights as "no rules" certainly attracted more spectators, but it also brought in as many detractors.

Enter into the fight a United States senator from Arizona, former Vietnam POW and all-around American hero, John McCain. Around 1996, Senator McCain and his Republicans, backed by Congress, decided to declare war on all things they deemed to be corroding the moral fabric of America's younger generation. The regular targets for moral outrage, such as rap music and sex, were always in the pockets of politicians seeking to stir voters, but this time around, the UFC provided the perfect example of the message they were trying to get across.

"Some of this is so brutal that it is nauseating," said McCain in an interview on *Larry King Live*, sitting beside fellow guests Ken Shamrock and UFC owner Bob Meyrowitz. "It appeals to the lowest common denominator in our society. This is something I think there is no place for," McCain added.

The world was not yet ready for the UFC, and crafty politicians took full advantage. Who wants to argue the merits of abortion, stricter environmental policy or better health care when you can get more attention attacking a sports event so blatantly violent? The carnage was there for everyone to see. Over and over again, politicians like McCain referenced the blood and gore of the UFC fights and followed by saying, "Is this the message we want to send to our kids?"

Spearheaded by McCain, the political action against the UFC started to pay dividends, and by 1996, Congress passed the V-Chip law that helped parents censor violent TV shows. This was one victory, but Senator McCain wanted to take the fight even further and have the UFC banned completely from all 50 states. He began a letter-writing campaign urging state governors to outright ban the UFC and any other event promoting such violence.

His strategy worked particularly well in 1995 in Wyoming (host of UFC 6) and in New York (host of UFC 7) later that year. Governors of both states agreed to ban any future events from being held on their watch. Even the tiny island territory of Puerto Rico was disgusted by the violence of ultimate fighting, and after the UFC 8 event in February 1996 was over, island officials barred any mixed martial arts tournaments from ever returning to their shores. Event lawyers had to go to court in Detroit and fight a battle of their own to make sure UFC 9 was allowed to go ahead as planned in that city.

UFC organizers tried to placate their critics by adding new rules, but the stigma still surrounding the sport had already sunk into the American public's perception of the events. The problem was that politicians like John McCain were selling lies and half-truths to the public and were ignorant of the many nuances in the sport. They pointed to the groin strikes, the graphic scenes of open wounds, the shots to the head and, one of the critics' main sticking points, the lack of protective gloves.

The point of reference for that last critique came from boxing. With padded gloves, a boxer could go 15 rounds without causing gaping wounds on his opponent's face. Boxing seemed safe to the layman, but barefisted fighting seemed barbaric. However, a closer look into the world of MMA reveals the huge differences between the two sports:

1. Boxing has a higher death rate per year than ultimate fighting. In sanctioned ultimate fights, there has only been a handful of deaths related to the sport. In 2007,

Houston, Texas, fighter Sam Vasquez died from a severe brain injury suffered during an October 20 Renegades Extreme Fighting Event. He had been hit only a few times by his opponent when he collapsed. The punches had burst a blood vessel in his brain, and Vasquez spent the next month in hospital before dying of his injuries.

In 2010, Michael Kirkham died in his Pro MMA debut as a result of the same injuries suffered by Vasquez. In a study done on boxing from 2000 to 2007, throughout the world, there averaged about 11 boxing-related deaths per year.

2. Ultimate fighting allows an athlete to tap out if he is injured or unable to continue, and doing so is not considered a cowardly act. In the boxing culture, to suddenly quit mid-fight is unheard of. Most boxers' only options are to win, fall unconscious or have their trainers throw in the towel. These dangerous options can lead to the fighter suffering unnecessary brain trauma, even though it is clear he will lose the fight in the end.

3. In ultimate fighting, gloves are worn to protect the fighter's hands. The thinly padded gloves allow for quick knockouts

and frequently cause bloody yet superficial injuries that lead to the stoppage of the fight. Although more padding might seem to better protect the opponent's head, the opposite outcome often occurs. Padded gloves allow the fighter to give more repetitive shots to the head that have a jarring effect on the brain, and over time, this can lead to more medical complications in athletes. And with padded gloves, athletes are more likely to swing with full power rather than go for a precision strike. Because of less padding in ultimate fighting gloves, the fighters have more options when it comes to ending a bout. In mixed martial arts, depending on the fighters, quite often not even a single punch will be thrown because the athletes use submission techniques as part of their weaponry in winning a fight.

4. The rounds in ultimate fighting are longer, which means that the fights are generally much shorter than in boxing, thereby decreasing the risk of injury in the short term, and in the long term over the course of a career. Also, in ultimate fighting, referees are given more power to intervene should they spot a fighter in trouble.

"In MMA, you're going to see there's more violence in their advertising and marketing, and to the casual observer it does seem more primitive and more violent," said Nick Lembo, counsel to the New Jersey State Athletic Control Board that officially sanctioned ultimate fighting in 2000. "But in terms of serious injuries, it seems safer than boxing."

Despite the facts, North American governments still believed that ultimate fighting had to be banned. In Canada, where several copycat organizations sprung up, organizers had the same amount of trouble as their U.S. counterparts in getting past the politicians. It came to the point where organizers had to host their events on Native reservations that were not subject to normal governmental laws and restrictions. The UFC and other ultimate fighting organizations attempted to appease the critics by instating new rules, such as banning groin shots and hair pulling and mandating that fighters wear protective gloves. The UFC even changed from its playoff-style format to weight divisions, as they do in boxing, starting at UFC 12, but the climate of hate toward MMA persisted.

It didn't help matters that the UFC events were becoming incredibly dull. As fast as the UFC created stars, the fighters would head across the Pacific to Japan, where Pride was paying handsome sums of money to their top fighters and where thousands of fans clamored to get into the arenas.

The Gracies had left after UFC 5 when Rorion sold his stake in the company, depriving the event of one of its biggest draws. Even UFC golden boy Ken Shamrock departed U.S. shores for the more lucrative Japanese market, and after his performance at UFC 9 in May 1996, no one blamed him.

Because of public pressure, UFC officials established a bunch of new rules that turned the event into a farce: closed-fisted strikes to the head and head butting were not allowed—rules that were followed up with threats by police to arrest any fighter who broke them. Some fighters still struck out with closed fists, and none were arrested, but in the Superfight between Dan Severn and Ken Shamrock, neither man wanted to take the chance. Shamrock had already been to jail and did not want to go back.

As a result of complying with the rules, the Severn-Shamrock Superfight was Superdull. The two fighters spent the majority of their half-hour battle simply circling each other as if they were dancing rather than fighting. They eventually wrestled a bit, but neither fighter seemed interested in the outcome, which Severn won via decision.

"Instead of engaging, taking the fight to him, I stood in the center of the ring while he circled around me...that was the most boring fight in UFC history, nothing more than a thirty-minute dance," said Shamrock.

After the politicians handcuffed the fighters from doing their job, they turned their attention to the cable companies and pay-per-view providers for allowing the dissemination of such violent programming. It did not help things that Senator John McCain had become chairman of the Commerce Committee, which was responsible for overseeing the proper conduct and regulation of the cable television industry. With that kind of power behind the lobby to rid the United States of ultimate fighting, the UFC was in a battle for survival.

The Los Angeles–based cable company TCI, which had over 14 million subscribers, halted all programming related to ultimate fighting in 1997. The newly appointed CEO of the company, Leo Hindery, proudly proclaimed in the *Los Angeles Times*, "I came here, found out where the bathrooms are, and cancelled Ultimate Fighting."

Time Warner cable quickly followed suit and cancelled their connections to the UFC. All of a sudden, the only way to see any of the UFC events was to have Direct TV satellite, and with the loss of viewers went the UFC's profits. Big-name fighters picked up and went to Japan. The UFC was in limbo and appeared on the brink of destruction.

The Return of the UFC

From the beginning of the UFC in 1993, it had no support. Semaphore Entertainment seemed to be fighting more battles in the courtroom to keep itself from fading off into the distance than athletes were fighting in the octagon. Ultimate fighting, simply put, needed a friend to help it out of a jam, someone with political or athletic clout that could help legitimize the sport. Every-one who took the time to get to know the sport could see its value. It was not the brutal, archaic, gladiatorial fight to the death that politicians were making it out to be. Albeit, the sport did not help itself by promoting in the "no holds barred," "two men enter, one man leaves" manner that it did. Good fighters like Ken Shamrock and Royce Gracie were proof that this was a legitimate sport with intelligent people behind it. Many support-ers of mixed martial arts fighting would point to Japan, where the Pride fights had become incredibly popular and where no one was ever severely injured, but ultimate fighting in North

America would continue to be a fringe sport until it was recognized by an official sanctioning body and given the credit it deserved.

The only two friends willing to hear the MMA fighters' case were the New Jersey State Athletic Commission and the Nevada State Athletic Commission. Both commissions were influential in American sports, and if UFC promoters could get either one on their side, the rest of the states were sure to, at the very least, take another look at the sport.

Semaphore took their case before the Nevada Commission and presented all sorts of facts, stats and rational arguments as to why the sport of MMA had a future in the state. According to Semaphore president Bob Meyrowitz, the meeting was going according to plan but was derailed at the last minute. Meyrowitz later claimed that the process was thrown by one commissioner in particular, casino magnate Lorenzo Fertitta, who would figure heavily in the future of the UFC. But a break for ultimate fighting would soon come.

While Semaphore knocked on doors and made phone calls in an effort to get its show back on television, rival MMA organization, the International Fighting Championships (IFC), went to the New Jersey Control Board and pleaded their case. Mixed martial arts finally ran into a friend, board chairman Larry Hazzard. Unlike its experience with most board members across the United States and similar governmental bodies in Canada, ultimate fighting had never come across anyone with the slightest knowledge of the sport, but Hazzard had a background in martial arts and understood the mentality of the athletes.

Hazzard knew that the majority of public opinion came from ignorance, and just as boxing had developed out of barefisted fighting bouts into a globally respected sport with rules and regulations, it was only a matter of time before the public and the politicians would see that mixed martial arts was a valid form of athletic competition. Hazzard granted the IFC his golden stamp of approval in 2000 and opened the door for all future MMA events and organizations. This ruling finally shed some light on the struggling UFC that was beginning to fade into non-existence— its events in southern states had attendances barely reaching 2000 and television audiences of about the same.

With such poor attendance figures, the UFC took its show abroad to Japan and Brazil and had some success, but the United States was its home, and with the ruling, everything began to change.

With the state of New Jersey behind it, Semaphore put on its first sanctioned show, UFC 28, in New Jersey on November 17, 2000, in Donald Trump's lavish Taj Mahal resort.

Semaphore was excited about the potential opportunities for the UFC, but it couldn't afford the high costs of the new venues in New Jersey and still had not brought the pay-per-view audiences back into the fold. Meyrowitz did not want to sell the entire operation outright, as he wanted to remain part of the company that he had spent years building. But after entertaining several offers, he knew that it was time to get out. The best offer, and the one that he accepted, came from Lorenzo Fertitta, who had turned him down to sanction the UFC in Nevada. Bad feelings aside, Meyrowitz knew that Fertitta had the right connections and the right people behind him to see that the UFC and mixed martial arts would survive and prosper, and that was his main concern in selling the company. In 2001, Semaphore sold its stake in UFC for a reported $2 million to the Zuffa Company, run by brothers Frank and Lorenzo Fertitta.

From the time that Lorenzo had turned down the UFC at the Nevada State Commission, he had taken it upon himself to learn more about the sport and even began his own Brazilian jiujitsu training. He learned to fight MMA style and finally understood that beyond the hype and publicity, this was an actual sport with a future.

"Once Lorenzo got involved, I think Bob (Meyrowitz) stepped back and said, 'You know what, this is something I've thrown a lot of money at, I've spent a lot of time with, and I don't want to see it die.' He sold it to the right people," said future UFC president Dana White. "You gotta give him credit for that."

The Rules

One of the most important factors in ultimate fighting receiving support of state athletic boards was the creation of the *Unified Rules of Mixed Martial Arts* in 2000 by the New Jersey State Athletic Commission. With this set of rules and regulations, the UFC and all other organizations could plead their case before other states and have a set of regulations that were followed across the sport. This rule book brought the legitimacy that the sport so desperately needed. The public and the politicians now were forced to look upon mixed martial arts as a new sport, a type of boxing for a new millennium. From the moment the rules were created, MMA went from being looked at as a bunch of bar-room brawlers to a proper codified athletic endeavor.

Some UFC Rules

1. Rounds were to be five minutes long with a one-minute rest in between. Non-title matches would go for three rounds while championship bouts were sanctioned for five rounds.

2. All athletes were required to wear approved shorts and no shoes or any other sort of foot padding. Shirts, gis or long pants were banned from competition. Fighters had to wear light gloves that allowed their fingers to grab. Competitors also had to wear a mouth guard and a jockstrap.

3. A 10-point judging system was put in place. Three judges decide the winner of each round, and at the end of the fight, if it was not decided via TKO or KO, the winner was the fighter with the most points.

4. In 2001, the Nevada State Athletic Commission added a list of fouls not to be committed:

   - Butting with the head
   - Eye gouging of any kind
   - Biting
   - Hair pulling

- Fish hooking (to insert the fingers into the mouth, nose or ears)
- Groin attacks of any kind
- Placing a finger into any orifice or into any laceration on an opponent
- Manipulation of fingers or toes
- Striking the spine or the back of the head
- Striking downward using the point of the elbow
- Throat strikes of any kind, including, without limitation, grabbing the trachea
- Clawing, pinching or twisting the flesh
- Grabbing the clavicle (considered to be gouging)
- Kicking the head of a grounded opponent
- Kneeing the head of a grounded opponent
- Stomping on a grounded opponent
- Kicking an opponent's kidney with the heel
- Spiking an opponent to the canvas on his head or neck
- Throwing an opponent out of the ring or fenced area
- Holding an opponent's shorts or gloves

- Spitting at an opponent
- Holding the ropes or the fence
- Using abusive language in the ring or fenced area
- Attacking an opponent during the break
- Attacking an opponent who is under the care of the referee
- Attacking an opponent after the bell (horn) has sounded the end of a round
- Flagrantly disregarding the instructions of the referee
- Timidity, including, without limitation, avoiding contact with an opponent, intentionally or consistently dropping the mouthpiece or faking an injury
- Interference by the corner

5. All fighters are regularly to be tested for steroids or other illegal or performance-enhancing drugs.

With a powerful, rich company now backing the sport, the sky was the limit for the UFC. After UFC 32 in June 2001, the cable companies and pay-per-view were once again on board, bringing back the fans and the desperately needed revenue. With the money now coming in, the UFC could finally afford to pay and keep the talented fighters who were beginning to make a name for themselves and who would soon propel mixed martial arts to a higher level. But as much as things began to change, the UFC needed something that would connect with a wider audience and give potential fans a way of getting to know the sport without committing to pay-per-view.

The Ultimate Fighter

Even after the Fertitta brothers took over ultimate fighting and dumped millions of dollars into the event, the UFC was still hemorrhaging money. The hardcore loyal fans who had adopted the UFC early on were not enough to sustain the multi-million-dollar franchise. The sport needed a new source of revenue and a new way to attract skeptical fans. The UFC owners decided that a reality television show might be the answer.

Boxing already had *The Contender*, and wrestling had *Tough Enough*, so the UFC jumped in with *The Ultimate Fighter*. After shopping the show around to a few cable stations, Spike TV was the first network to jump on board. The station's main audience was young men from 16 to 40 years of age, and what better way to increase viewership than with a reality show about ultimate fighting?

The UFC was becoming a brand, and the television show aided in selling its product. When it first came out in 1993, the UFC really only sought to answer the question of what martial art would be the best in a fight. UFC promoters had never envisioned creating a whole new sport unto itself, but if the brand UFC was to survive, it needed to produce a grassroots movement that interested a younger generation. A reality-based TV program about up-and-coming ultimate fighters would be a perfect way to introduce people to the fighter's world and show the human face of a sport that so many people had said lacked humanity.

The premise of the show was to stick two teams of eight fighters in a house and follow them as they trained and fought through the competition for the prized contract with the UFC. The men were placed under the guidance of a recognized UFC star as their coach. Each member of a team would compete against a member of the other team until a champion was proclaimed in a final match-up.

The first season of the reality program in 2005 was a huge success for the UFC and Spike television, and the finale drew millions of viewers. But more importantly, the final fight of season one was the first time in mixed martial arts history that an event was seen on a live, open television network. UFC president Dana White said that the final fight between Stephan Bonnar and Forrest Griffin saved the UFC by bringing the sport into the homes of millions of people who had never seen or knew nothing about MMA. Articles were written in newspapers that had never before bothered to report anything about the UFC unless it was something negative.

With each season of *The Ultimate Fighter*, the ratings only grew. The show brought in new fans and was the perfect platform for the introduction of new stars. The first season ended a week prior to the airing of UFC 52, and because of the reality show, the event had unprecedented coverage. The venue, MGM Grand Garden Arena on the Las Vegas strip, had sold all its 14,562 seats to see Chuck Liddell take on Randy Couture for the championship in April 2005, and close to 300,000 people signed up to the pay-per-view event on TV. Compare that with UFC 50, where only 9000 people attended the fight and 40,000 people subscribed to pay-per-view.

In a few short years, Zuffa and the brains behind the new UFC had completely turned a losing enterprise into one of the fastest growing sports. Stadiums now sell out, and pay-per-view audiences can number in the millions for the more popular fighters. And with some rule changes, even the harshest of critics softened up. "They have cleaned up the sport to the point, at least in my view, where it is not human cockfighting any more. I think they've made significant progress. They haven't made me a fan, but they have made progress," said U.S. Senator John McCain.

Top Five All-time Greatest Fighters in MMA History

It's only after we've lost everything that we're free to do anything.

–Tyler Durden (Brad Pitt), in the film *Fight Club*

Author's note: This was not an easy list to compile, given the number of great fighters out there in the world. I did consider doing a top 10 or 15 list, but with all the different weight classes and different MMA networks, it was difficult to know where to begin. So I have compiled a random list of the fighters who, I believe, have made the greatest impact inside the ring or octagon. Although some great fighters have surely been left out (the stories of the Gracies and Ken Shamrock have already been told), I'm confident that you'll have a hard time disagreeing with the ones on this list.

Fedor Emelianenko (aka The Last Emperor)

Outside the ring, Fedor Emelianenko is a soft-spoken, humble man. Inside the ring, any fighter will tell you he was one of the greatest mixed martial artists of all time. But his career began more out of necessity than out of a love for fighting.

After putting in his time with the Russian army as a military firefighter from 1995 to 1997, Emelianenko was released and found there were not many jobs for someone with his particular set of skills. He had learned judo and its Russian offshoot, sambo, in the military and had proven to be adept at the martial arts. He used these skills to join the Russian national judo team and won several medals at competitions and at World Cup events. Earning that spot on the team and winning the medals was a great source of pride, but the pay was not enough to support his young family. That is when he heard of the Rings fighting network coming out of Japan.

Emelianenko made his debut in Rings against Tsuyoshi Kohsaka at the King of Kings event in 2000. But the fight was marred by controversy. Rings rules did not allow the use of elbow strikes to the head unless the striker was wearing elbow pads, and at just the 17-second mark of the fight,

Kohsaka missed on a punch and caught Emelianenko with his elbow, opening up a huge cut on his forehead. The referee did not see the illegal elbow and declared Kohsaka the winner by default.

It was a horrible way to start a career in professional fighting, but Emelianenko would not disappoint in any of his subsequent fights, not losing another match while fighting under the Rings promotion. In February 2002, he defeated Chris Haseman to win the last tournament ever held by the Rings promotion. It folded a few months later.

With the money and offers steadily pouring in, Emelianenko joined the Pride Fighting Championships, making his debut at Pride 21 on June 23, 2002. When he first joined the Pride network, not many people had given him credit for being a good fighter. He had no training in Brazilian jiujitsu, and as Rings was often criticized for their fights being on the timid side because of the amount of regulations and the fact that some of the fights were fixed, fighters who came out of that tradition were not looked upon as much of a threat to the "tougher" Pride fighters.

The first unlucky Pride fighter of note to taste what Emelianenko had to offer was 6-foot-4 Heath Herring. Going into the fight, Herring had

Ground and pound is a fundamental technique in MMA in which a grappler secures a mount position on his opponent and then delivers punches, elbows and kicks with impunity.

been the odds-on-favorite to win because of his size and ferocity in the ring. The bout winner would face Antonio Rodrigo Nogueira for the heavyweight championship. In the fight, the world got to see just how brutal a fighter Fedor Emelianenko could be with his skilled ground and pound technique.

From the moment the bell sounded the fight's start, Emelianenko dominated. Herring came at him with a flying front kick, which Emelianenko caught and then used as leverage to throw Herring to the ground. From there, Emelianenko mercilessly beat on Herring, who had to throw himself partially out of the ring simply to stop the onslaught. But when the fight resumed, Emelianenko got him to the ground again and was able to choke Herring out for the win.

Next up for Emelianenko was the title bout against Nogueira at Pride 25 on March 16, 2003, a match that would make the Russian a legend. Nogueira was a noted technical master of Brazilian jiujitsu and was not easily defeated. The remarkable thing about Emelianenko was that he never looked fazed or intimidated by any of his opponents, never once retreating from an attack. You could see this in the first few seconds of the fight.

At the sound of the bell, the two fighters moved forward, dancing about, looking for their first opening. Emelianenko kept his eyes trained on the Brazilian, never once stepping back. Nogueira did not seem to know what to make of Emelianenko's challenges and stepped back every time he advanced. Not one to wait for his opponent to make a move, Emelianenko took the first swing and connected a devastating right hand to Nogueira's jaw that forced the Brazilian to step back against the ropes in a daze. Emelianenko ended up on top of Nogueira and used his ground and pound skills to gut-wrenching effect. The jiujitsu artist skilled in the technical side of fighting seemed at a loss with what to do against such a formidable force. He managed to mount Emelianenko from the top, but the slippery Russian reversed the maneuver and continued his onslaught of punches from above.

For three brutal rounds, Emelianenko dominated the Brazilian with his hard ground and pound style. Nogueira tried everything he could from the guard position—arm bars, leg locks and flying kicks—but Emelianenko seemed to be one step ahead of his opponent the entire time. After the set three rounds, Nogueira fell into the arms of one of his coaches and waited for the inevitable judges' decision in the fight. Emelianenko had won the heavyweight Pride championship belt and had placed himself on the map as one of the greatest fighters in mixed martial arts.

But by no means was Fedor Emelianenko completely untouchable in a fight. Over the next 16 Pride fights, he got himself into trouble several times but somehow always seemed to come out the winner. Even when he ate a huge right hand from Kazuyuki Fujita that had Emelianenko wobbling around the ring with his arms failing, he still managed to hold his ground and come back in the fight two minutes later, beating Fujita with a rear naked choke.

In a fight against Kevin Randleman, Emelianenko was picked up by Randleman and back suplexed on his head, a move that would usually bring out the doctors, but Emelianenko came back and finished Randleman off with a Kimura arm lock. In all of his fights, Emelianenko was a man possessed; no fighter was able to match his intensity, skill and sheer toughness.

After the death of Pride fighting because of its alleged ties to the Japanese mafia, Emelianenko went back to Russia to fight in the new Bodog-Fight events started by billionaire Calvin Ayre. Emelianenko faced American Matt Lindland in front of Russian president Vladimir Putin, Italian prime minister Silvio Berlusconi and action star Jean-Claude Van Damme. After defeating Lindland with an arm bar in the first round, barely even taking a punch in the fight, Emelianenko spent the rest of the night with the two politicians and Van Damme at the Presidential Palace.

With his incredible record and explosive star power, there was nobody the UFC wanted more than Fedor Emelianenko. UFC president Dana

White made it his mission to bring the Russian into his company and fight under his banner. The idea was to have a heavyweight fight against then-UFC champion Randy Couture. White offered Emelianenko somewhere in the neighborhood of one million dollars to join the UFC, but Emelianenko's management team began making crazy demands, including the building of a stadium in Russia.

The two sides could not come to an agreement, so Emelianenko joined the new fighting network Affliction, where he fought against former UFC champions Kevin Randleman, Mark Coleman and Andrei Arlovski and defeated all three. After the Affliction network folded, the UFC made another attempt at signing Emelianenko, this time to fight heavyweight Brock Lesnar, but again, millions of dollars were passed up because of the crazy demands of Emelianenko's inept management. Instead, Emelianenko joined Strikeforce, and it was announced that he would have his first fight broadcast nationally on CBS television against then-undefeated Brett Rogers on November 7, 2009. Emelianenko won that fight via TKO in the second round.

Emelianenko suffered his first real loss in 10 years (the first recorded loss of his MMA career was doctor stoppage because of blood) when he went up against Brazilian Fabricio Werdum and was submitted via arm bar at just 1:09 of the first round. It was a tough loss for his fans to accept, but the quiet Russian looked at the loss rather philosophically, saying, "The one who doesn't fall never stands up. It happened that people made me an idol. But everybody loses. I'm just a human being. And if it's God's will, next fight, I'll win."

But what Emelianenko did not tell anyone was that he was considering retirement from the world of fighting. At 34 years of age, he was beginning to deteriorate, and the injuries were mounting. The MMA world was relieved to hear that Emelianenko had agreed to another fight, set to take place on February 12, 2011, in New Jersey against Antonio "Bigfoot" Silva.

After a close first round, Silva took control of the fight in the second, landing a series of hard punches from the mount. For the second time in his career, Emelianenko looked like he could not find his way out of something. Silva's punches never knocked him out or forced him to submit, but they did cause Emelianenko's eye to swell shut, forcing doctors to give Silva the win by default.

After the fight, Emelianenko announced to the crowd that the fight had been his last.

But upon returning to Russia, he told the press that he might come back, given the proper circumstances. Whether or not Fedor Emelianenko returns, he will forever be one of the deadliest fighters ever to step into a ring.

Georges St-Pierre (aka GSP, aka Rush)

Apart from only a handful of fighters, maybe even just one other, no one has dominated mixed martial arts the way Saint-Isodore, Quebec, native Georges St-Pierre has since first breaking into the sport in 2002 with Montreal's TKO Major League MMA. Just two fights into his career, he had already become the local champion. But St-Pierre was not always the toughest guy around.

As a boy growing up in the small town of Saint-Isodore, he was often the target of neighborhood bullies. He was smaller than the rest of the kids, and he knew that the only way he would be able to stand up to the bullies was to learn how to defend himself against any size of opponent. Luckily, in his town lived a karate instructor named Jean Couture who took St-Pierre under his wing and made sure he learned the necessary tools of defense.

But in 1993 when the first UFC came out, St-Pierre was transfixed on the event and on one fighter in particular: Royce Gracie. St-Pierre, like many others of his generation, was curious about Gracie's style of fighting and how it could completely dominate against much larger opponents. An amateur chess player, St-Pierre saw the art of strategy in a fight and immediately began to learn jiujitsu. He knew that he was meant to fight in the UFC, and he set his sights on the big time. While going to school and training in boxing, wrestling and jiujitsu, to make ends meet, he had several odd jobs, including working as a bouncer in a suburban Montreal bar and as a garbage man for several weeks. Working at bars and odd jobs was not something St-Pierre wanted to do forever. He looked to the MMA world for his way out.

St-Pierre got his start in the MMA world in 2000 when he joined the Urban Conflict Championship (UCC) fighting network. In all five of his UCC fights, St-Pierre never lost and never took a fight past the second round. He was willing to put in his time in the smaller MMA events, but he always wanted to compete in the UFC.

Two years later, at just 22 years of age, he made his debut at UFC 46, fighting Karo Parisyan in the welterweight division. St-Pierre proved to be better technically and came out on top, winning by unanimous decision. That same night after his fight, St-Pierre sat and watched as two fighters, who would later figure predominantly in his rise to the top, battled for the welterweight championship. Matt Hughes had gone two years without a single loss and looked to be unbeatable, but his challenger, B.J. Penn, had a powerful punch and an unpredictable style. Penn managed to knock Hughes sideways with a powerful right hand and then finished him off with a rear naked choke for the championship win.

Watching on the sideline, St-Pierre knew he would have to train hard to win that title, but he never doubted he could. Shortly after that event, Penn was stripped of his title when he breached his contract with the UFC by fighting in a rival league, and again Matt Hughes was declared champion. Suddenly, the UFC needed a challenger for Hughes, and St-Pierre got the call he had been waiting for.

St-Pierre was shocked at suddenly being thrust into the ring with a fighter he greatly admired—he could barely even look at Hughes as referee John McCarthy went through the pre-fight instructions at UFC 50, in October 2004. St-Pierre managed to hold his own in the fight but could not seem to get past the enormity of fighting Matt Hughes for the championship belt after only one fight in the UFC. The crowd thought an upset was in the making when St-Pierre landed a swift kick to Hughes' midsection, but Hughes returned by slamming the rookie into the ground. With the seconds ticking off the end of the first round, St-Pierre made a rookie mistake against a wily veteran in attempting a poorly executed Kimura arm lock, which Hughes turned into an arm lock of his own, ending the fight with just one second left in the round. It was a hard lesson for St-Pierre to learn, but a necessary one.

He would have to earn his way back to the title like the rest of the fighters. One by one, he dispatched every challenger, including the certifiably insane Jason Miller, who laughed and smiled his way through a beating by St-Pierre that lasted three rounds. Then came wins against skilled fighters Dave Strasser, Frank Trigg and Sean Sherk, before beating B.J. Penn for the right to his second shot at Matt Hughes and the Welterweight Championship at UFC 65 in November 2006.

St-Pierre worked tirelessly in training for his rematch with Hughes—his boxing, his grappling and his physical stamina all were in peak shape by the time he stepped in the ring. But most importantly, he was mentally ready. He had studied Hughes in order to learn his weaknesses, and he believed he could take him down.

The win against Hughes has been the greatest moment of St-Pierre's career to date, and he reveled in the glow of the golden belt. But the glory did not last long. Just a few months later, he lost the belt to Matt Serra. It was one of the most stunning upsets in UFC history. Serra had never really made much of an impression in his previous fights, and going into his battle with St-Pierre, he was considered at 12–1 odds to actually win.

The match at UFC 69 in April 2007 started out with St-Pierre taking control of the fight with a wicked jab that caught Serra several times, sending the decidedly pro-St-Pierre crowd into a frenzy. But just a few minutes later, Serra managed to connect with a heavy right-hander that surely clouded St-Pierre's vision, catching him on the side of the head. Serra jumped on the opportunity and rained punches down on the dazed Canadian fighter, forcing him to tap out.

The sudden loss of his title was hard for St-Pierre to swallow, but it made him more determined than ever to return to the octagon and claim what he felt was rightfully his. "In my career, there have been two great turning points," said St-Pierre. "The first is when I lost to Matt Hughes and the second is when I lost to Serra. After those losses, I made a lot of changes in my training, my entourage, and everything in my life. I become better after every fight, but after these two losses I became way better."

With his mind and body refocused, St-Pierre returned to the octagon and completely dominated all opponents. He easily defeated wrestling pro Josh Koscheck, then defeated rival Matt Hughes, before finally making it back to fight Matt Serra to reclaim his title before a packed Bell Centre in his home province in Montreal, Quebec, in April 2008. St-Pierre had trained hard for this fight and used his technical prowess in grappling and wrestling to halt any attempts by Serra to mount an offense. By the second round, the fight was halted by the referee because Serra had remained on the defensive the entire fight and did not even attempt to make any sort of maneuver to escape St-Pierre's attacks. St-Pierre had reclaimed his title and has not parted with it since. Josh Koscheck returned to fight again, but St-Pierre easily beat him. Thiago Alves came close, but despite a tear in his groin, St-Pierre won that fight as well.

In the welterweight division, it would seem no fighters are left for St-Pierre to battle because his dominance of the sport has been so complete. Before Jake Shields and St-Pierre even stepped into the octagon, several sports pundits were saying that Shields might be able to remove St-Pierre from his throne, but their battle at UFC 129 in April 2011 proved that St-Pierre would never give up in a fight, despite having one eye swollen shut for most of the match. There have been rumors of moving St-Pierre up a division to face heavier fighters, or maybe even fighting middleweight fighting ace Anderson Silva, but nothing has yet been worked out. For now, St-Pierre is just happy being champion.

Anderson Silva

As Georges St-Pierre has dominated the welterweight division of the UFC, so too has Brazilian-born Anderson Silva dominated the middleweight division. In fact, he is the UFC's longest reigning champion, currently having 13 consecutive wins.

Primarily a muay thai fighter, Anderson Silva is also well versed in Brazilian jiujitsu, taekwondo, judo and capoeira, making him a deadly versatile fighter. But when he began his fighting career, he had not yet attained the level of greatness that he currently holds. He first made his name known in the Cage Rage organization with several jaw-dropping knockouts, including the ridiculous reverse upper cut elbow on Tony Fryklund. When standing up in a fight, Silva was without a doubt one of the most creative and dangerous fighters in the ring, but if an opponent managed to get him to the ground, he never looked like he knew what he was doing and often was beaten by less than stellar fighters.

One of his most embarrassing losses came at the hands of Ryo Chonan in a Pride fight in December 2004. Throughout the entire fight, Silva was dominating with vicious punches and a muay thai–style knee to the head for which Chonan had no defense. It seemed just a matter of connecting at the right time and Chonan would get knocked out. With nothing else to lose, Chonan tried his luck with a flying scissor heel hook and managed to get Silva to tap out. Chonan could hardly believe the move had worked, but it proved that Silva had a long way to go before he could be considered one of the best.

Silva realized that if he wanted to attain the heights of the prizefighting world, he would need to diversify his attack to avoid future embarrassing losses to lesser opponents. He began training in Brazilian jiujitsu under the watchful eye of Antonio Rodrigo Nogueira, and in 2006, he earned his black belt in the discipline. Learning jiujitsu was the best thing Silva could have done for his career. In that same year, he joined the UFC and would fight brawler Chris Leben.

Leben was a good all-round fighter who had come out of *The Ultimate Fighter* reality TV series school of fighting. He walked into the ring brimming with confidence and expecting to meet the same inconsistent Anderson Silva who lost against lesser fighters. Silva started out his UFC career in June 2006 by completely dominating his fight against Leben, dispelling any ideas that he was an inconsistent fighter. In just 49 seconds, Silva knocked Leben out cold with a perfect display of boxing skills that had rarely been seen in the UFC.

After that one fight, Silva was thrown directly into a championship match against Rich Franklin at UFC 64 in October 2006. The fight marked Silva's arrival into the realm of one of the greatest UFC middleweight bouts. For two minutes straight, Silva attacked with flurries of knees, kicks and jabs that kept Franklin dazed and incapable of countering. Silva finished off the one-sided fight with a straight knee to Franklin's head that pushed his nose over to the side of his face. Since that fight, Silva has not had a significant challenge to his title.

But the Brazilian has had his fair share of controversy. At UFC 112 in Abu Dhabi in April 2010, held outdoors for the first time in UFC history, Anderson Silva put on one of his most controversial performances. He appeared somewhat bored by his challenger Demian Maia and taunted him by dancing around the octagon, shooting in straight jabs but never going in for the knockout punch. In the third and fourth rounds of the bout, Silva completely removed himself from the fight and simply danced about the octagon waiting for Maia to make a move. These actions angered the fans, who were looking for a typical action-packed Silva fight. The referee was forced to stop the fight in the fifth round and give Silva a warning for his lack of effort and disrespectful conduct.

Without any flair or action, the fight ended, and Silva was declared the winner via unanimous decision, but no one in the arena that day was happy about his performance. UFC president Dana White walked out on the fight in the fourth round and refused to return to place the championship belt around Silva's waist.

After the fight, everyone in the MMA world was wondering about Silva's level of commitment to the sport and whether he even cared about defending his title. Dana White went so far as to say in an interview, "If he [Silva] ever acts like that again in the ring, I will cut him."

For his return fight, Anderson Silva was put up against the beefy Chael Sonnen in UFC 117 on August 7, 2010. Right from the opening bell, Silva did not look as spry as he had in his previous fights, taking several hard punches to the head and body from Sonnen before getting taken down to the ground where the championship hopeful continued to pound on a helpless Silva.

The Brazilian managed to survive, but the following rounds continued in much of the same fashion, and if he didn't do something quick, Silvia was in danger of losing his title. With just three minutes left in the bout, a tired and worn-out-looking Silva managed to lock Sonnen up in a triangle arm bar and force him to submit. It has been reported that Silva went into the fight with a rib injury despite doctors warning him not to step in the ring. It turned out that he had injured that rib in the fight with Sonnen and was forced to remain out of the UFC until early 2011.

Silva's first fight back on the UFC tour put him up against Vitor Belfort on February 5, 2011, at UFC 126. No one knew how Silva would react after being out of the octagon for so long, but he had not lost his trademark flair for the dramatic and ended the fight just three minutes into the first round with a vicious front kick to the jaw that sent Belfort reeling, followed by a barrage of punches that forced the referee to stop the fight.

Opponent after opponent, Silva has proven that he is one of the greatest fighters in the UFC. All recent challengers have been sent back to the training room, and not one fighter has been able to show the world that he could beat him in combat; all this and Silva is 36 years old. With nothing left to prove in the octagon, Silva has often publicly hinted at retirement and has frequently spoken of his desire to step into a different ring and fight boxer Roy Jones Jr. on his turf. Having won 13 consecutive MMA fights, and with his legendary status already secure in the UFC, no one could blame Silva for seeking out new challenges.

Randy Couture (aka Captain America)

Despite Randy Couture's career record of 19 wins and 11 losses, he has done more to popularize the sport of MMA and the UFC than most fighters with far better records. When Couture joined the UFC in 1997, it was still a fringe sport that operated in dark, smoky and thinly populated arenas in the southern U.S. The life was not glamorous at all, but it was the challenge of proving himself that brought Couture to the octagon. When he first stepped into the ring, people were doubtful that he could succeed because, at the age of 34, many did not think he could last against a well-trained 25-year-old. But with age comes wisdom and experience.

Couture had been a devoted practitioner of Greco-Roman wrestling since his teenage years in his home state of Washington. If that did not make him tough enough, after he finished school, he joined the U.S. Army for six years. Upon returning home, he continued his wrestling career, becoming a three-time Olympic team alternate and winning a gold medal at the 1991 Pan American Games in the 90-kilogram (198-pound) Greco-Roman wrestling event. Life as an amateur wrestler was fun for Couture, but it didn't bring in a lot of money, so after the 1996 Olympic Games, Couture settled into a life as a wrestling coach.

He would have continued his teaching career had he not seen a video of a UFC event and become hooked on the energy of the sport. The old wrestler inside of him awoke at the thought of putting his skills to the test in an arena with no rules. At UFC 13 in May 1997, he would get his chance to show just what he was capable of.

For his first fight, Couture was thrown in the ring with Tony Halme, also known as World Wrestling Federation wrestler Ludvig Borga, who outweighed Couture by 100 pounds. It would be a great physical and mental challenge for Couture—who was used to going up against opponents at least in the same weight class—but the early days of the UFC thrived on unpredictability, and it was anyone's guess what the outcome would be.

Just a few seconds into the fight, Couture got things started with a double-leg takedown. He then worked a vigorous ground and pound, forcing Halme to give up his back for the (relatively) easy rear naked choke win in just under a minute. Couture fought a second time that night with similar results, beating Steven Graham in the tournament finals a little over three minutes into the first round.

Randy Couture had arrived. He had shown all the doubters that age did not matter. It was about training and using your knowledge to take down an opponent anyway possible. Most importantly,

DOUBLE-LEG TAKEDOWN

One of the most basic but important takedown techniques in a fighter's weaponry, the move is secured by shooting in below the opponent's waist, grabbing both his legs and using your momentum to take him to the ground.

he had proven to himself that he could survive in the arena. Now he set his sights on the top prize: the heavyweight championship belt.

Yet before he could do that, he had to fight his way through a young up-and-comer named Vitor Belfort, who had been making waves in recent fights by knocking out opponents with powerful strikes and smart submissions. In his mid-30s, Couture would be in tough against the 20-year-old Belfort, who, besides the age difference, was a Gracie jiujitsu black belt, a power puncher and had even found time to schedule in a trial to be on the Brazilian Olympic boxing team.

On October 7, 1997, at UFC 15, Couture put on a display that earned him his well-deserved reputation as a masterful technical and strategic fighter. It was obvious from the opening rounds of the fight that Belfort wanted to take the old man down with one of his patented power strikes to the face, but Couture had watched Belfort's tapes and was well prepared for anything the Brazilian was ready to throw his way. Every time Belfort would go for the strikes to the head, Couture would nimbly fall beneath the blows and shoot in for a takedown. A few takedowns failed, but when Couture succeeded in getting Belfort to the ground, he would manage to gain the mount and work him down slowly with punches and knee strikes. When the referee brought them back to their feet, Couture did not want to risk another takedown attempt against the black belted jiujitsu skills of Belfort and decided to play with the young fighter by standing up to him and boxing it out.

Although Belfort was a trained boxer, he had always gained control in standup fights early on. By the five-minute mark of the first round, he had already burned through so much energy just trying to stay on his feet and defend against Couture's strategic attacks that his most devastating weapon had been rendered weak and ineffectual. After a few minutes of clutch-and-grab boxing, Belfort could not defend against another takedown. Couture finished the fight off with a flood of strikes from the back mount before the referee had seen his share of violence and declared Couture the winner.

Next up for Couture was a shot at the heavyweight title against champion Maurice Smith at UFC Japan just two months after his fight with Belfort. The title fight, however, was not the most exciting bout in UFC history.

Smith had done his homework on Couture as any good champion would, and he knew that he was in for a chess match of a fight. Neither fighter really went on the offensive, and much of the match was spent jockeying for position and looking to score points with the judges. Couture managed to impress the judges with a few takedowns and his positional control on the ground. After 21 minutes, the two tired heavyweights were separated, and Couture was declared the winner via majority decision, making him the new heavyweight champion.

Now with the title in hand, Couture was faced with a whole host of other fighters waiting in the wings ready to strip him of his belt. In 1998, organizers of the UFC wanted Couture to fight Bas Rutten for the championship title. It was going to be the premiere fight at the next UFC, but Couture had different plans. At that time, the UFC was not the multi-million-dollar business that it is today. Fighters did not earn nearly the same amount as they do now, and many simply left for greener pastures elsewhere.

Couture decided to sign on with Vale Tudo Japan for more money than the UFC was offering and ended up forfeiting his title. After bouncing around several organization for a few years, he eventually returned to the UFC in 2000, when he defeated heavyweight title holder Kevin Randleman to reclaim the title he had left behind three years earlier.

During his three-year absence, much had changed in the UFC. It was now under new management, and many of the new fighters were well versed in the art of combat. The UFC was no longer an arena for guys looking to show the world how tough they were; it was now a place where dedicated athletes featured skills they had been working on for years. In addition, Couture was no longer a young man. In 2003, he was about to turn 40, and the prospect of fighting heavier, younger guys did not appeal to him or represent the career path he wanted. To level the playing field, he dropped a few pounds and moved into the light heavyweight division.

The light heavyweight division had long been dominated by Tito Ortiz, and, looking for a headline event, UFC president Dana White wanted Ortiz to go up against Chuck Liddell in a title fight. Ortiz claimed that he did not want to fight Liddell because they had once been training partners, and he pulled out of a possible match. (In fact, Ortiz was involved in a contract negotiation with the UFC and would not fight until it was resolved.) To fill the vacant fight card, White pushed Couture into the ring to face Liddell for the interim championship title.

Despite his championship background in the heavyweight division, Couture was again saddled with the underdog label before the fight, given his age and the fact that Liddell had won several of his fights in devastating fashion against tough opponents. Many MMA writers had written off Couture even before Liddell finished his grand theatrical entrance to the music of Vanilla Ice's "Ice Ice Baby." However, being the underdog suited Couture just fine.

In the first and second rounds, Couture used his boxing skills to stand up against Liddell, avoiding any of his knockout swings and keeping him at bay with precise jabs. By the third round, Liddell had exhausted himself, giving Couture the opening he needed. Moving in for the take-down, Couture gained position on Liddell and threw punches at him until the referee stopped the fight for the TKO. Couture was again, against all odds, champion.

Randy Couture would continue to fight, winning and losing fights over the next few years, and though he was no longer the dominant fighter who came into the UFC as a complete unknown, he went into each fight and gave every ounce of energy he had against guys half his age. His final fight was against Lyoto Machida at UFC 129 in April 2011 before a crowd of 55,700 spectators. Couture lost the fight in the second round after receiving a vicious front kick that looked very similar to the move that Daniel San used in the final scene of the *Karate Kid* movie. It was immediately after the fight that he announced to the crowd that he was "finally done fighting." Throughout his career, Couture never backed down in a fight, gave everything he had, and, outside of the octagon, was one of the sport's greatest ambassadors.

Matt Hughes

Born in the sleepy town of Hillsboro, Illinois, Matt Hughes got his start in the athletic world playing football and wrestling in school. Although he enjoyed football, wrestling was his passion. During high school he won two state championships, in 1990 and 1991. After finishing college, Hughes was coaching at a local college and earning his electrician apprenticeship on the side when a friend approached him with the idea to fight for real, not wrestle, in a small local event. Hughes tried it out and became hooked on the adrenaline rush of mixed martial arts. After a few more fights in MMA competitions, Hughes made his way to Japan, where he slowly began to make a name for himself as one of the next fighters to watch.

With a career record of 45 wins and eight losses, Matt Hughes definitely earned his spot in the UFC Hall of Fame to which he was inducted in May 2010. With such a history, you would figure that at the beginning of his career, fans would have flocked to arenas around the country to see him, but many people considered his fights simply boring. He had no flair for the dramatic, did not enter the ring with music and smoke like Chuck Liddell and was every bit the respectful Midwesterner stereotype in interviews. His penchant for taking opponents down early in fights and keeping them there until he gained control was technically sound but boring for fans.

Just when his career seemed to be fading off into the distance, he appeared on the second season of *The Ultimate Fighter* and began to fully appreciate the marketing potential to becoming a villainous character in the UFC. Hughes became just as cocky as Tito Ortiz, mocking his opponents before fights and making grandiose statements about how great a fighter he was. The thing about Matt Hughes was that it was not all just talk—he had the skills to back up every claim.

He slowly worked his way through a list of fighters before finally getting his chance at the UFC welterweight title, taking on Carlos Newton in what would become one of the most memorable fights in the organization's history. The fight, part of UFC 34 on November 2, 2001, started out as expected, with a few early punches and a close battle on the ground. Both Hughes and Newton were excellent submission fighters, and the better part of the first round and the opening minutes of the second round were spent in a strategic lockup on the ground, with both men trying to position themselves for a submission hold.

Around the three-minute mark of the second round, Newton managed to secure a triangle choke on Hughes by wrapping his legs around his head. In a desperate attempt to free himself, in an incredible feat of Herculean strength, Hughes lifted his opponent off the ground while Newton still held on firmly around his neck. Despite being lifted into the air, Newton tightened his triangle choke, but Hughes refused to submit. Hughes had only one option. He slammed his attacker to the ground, causing Newton to lose consciousness. The referee immediately broke up the fight and declared a dazed Hughes the winner.

After the match, Newton claimed that the only reason Hughes slammed him to the ground was because he had lost consciousness himself from the triangle choke. Although Hughes refused to admit it publicly, in tapes of the fight, Hughes can be heard telling his corner after the fight, "I was out. I was out." Despite the circumstances,

Hughes was the new welterweight champion and had made a name for himself among the best fighters in the world.

He would go on to defeat such notable fighters as Frank Trigg, Sean Sherk, B.J. Penn and Royce Gracie, and he handed Georges St-Pierre one of his only two career losses. By the time St-Pierre got his revenge on Hughes at UFC 65 to claim the championship title, Hughes wasn't the same fighter he used to be. When he first entered mixed martial arts fighting back in 1998, he had relied on being stronger and faster than his opponents, and when age began to take that away, it was easy to see that he was not a prime contender in the UFC. He won and lost a few more fights, but the skilled fighter who once got the crowds to their feet was no longer there, and many people began to wonder if Matt Hughes could remain relevant in the UFC. Although he can still bring in the diehard fans, it is doubtful that he will ever be able to reclaim any championship titles.

Honorable Mention: Tito Ortiz

As much as people like to hate Tito Ortiz, whose real name is Jacob Ortiz, it's hard to dispute that he was one of the most dynamic and entertaining fighters in UFC history. He was an explosive fighter in the octagon, with powerful fists that, if they connected, were known to knock a few opponents senseless. His fighting style was erratic and undisciplined, but he made up for his lack of refinement with pure energy. With Ortiz there was no middle ground; you either loved him or hated him.

Before all the fighting, the hype and the many feuds, Ortiz seemed destined to a different career path, getting a college degree and focusing his natural athletic talents on amateur wrestling. Then one day, the direction of his life took a sudden turn when UFC bad boy Tank Abbott asked him to be his training partner. Ortiz accepted and got pulled into a career that would see him make a meteoric rise to the top of the MMA world in a short amount of time.

Seeing the potential in the young Ortiz, UFC organizers offered to sign him to fight in UFC 13 in 1997, but because he was still in college, he was not eligible for the professional contract. This did nothing to deter Ortiz. He didn't care about the money and signed on anyway as an amateur. In his first UFC fight that May, he pummeled Wes Albritton into submission in just 31 seconds of the first round.

Ortiz's confidence continued to grow from that fight as he set higher sights for himself. One thing he understood very well from the beginning was that the UFC was a business, and by playing a certain role for the cameras and the audience, he was guaranteed to bring more visibility to the sport. He wore T-shirts that mocked his opponents, he entered the ring wearing vampire teeth and he generally did everything he could to get attention, whether good or bad. Along the way, his behavior earned him as many enemies as fans.

One of the most notable feuds that developed in Ortiz's career was his public war of words in the media and in the ring with Ken Shamrock. It all started in 1999 when Ortiz beat Shamrock protégé Guy Mezger at UFC 19 and immediately after the fight put on a T-shirt that read, "Gay Mezger Is My Bitch." Shamrock, who was in Mezger's corner for that fight, jumped onto the fence of the octagon and screamed for Ortiz to remove the offensive shirt while of course hurling expletives of all kinds.

It was the start of a feud that would eventually lead to Shamrock and Ortiz meeting at UFC 40 three years after the initial spark. This was one of the most anticipated fights in UFC history. The pay-per-view buy rate was nearly four times higher than the previous record, and attention for the event was even beginning to bleed into mainstream media. Prior to the fight, both Ortiz and Shamrock appeared on ESPN's *The Best Damn Sports Show Period* and engaged in a lively trash talk session.

However, when the two finally got into the ring, it was Ortiz who was able to back up his words the best by dominating the fight both standing up and on the ground. By the third round, Shamrock was tired, bruised and bloody, and before the referee could call the fighters back for the fourth round, Shamrock's corner threw in the towel. If Ortiz was confident before the fight, he was absolutely shining bright after beating Shamrock.

Now holder of the light heavyweight title and having just defeated golden boy Ken Shamrock, Ortiz felt he needed to receive the compensation he rightly deserved from the UFC. This was a business, and as the top fighter in the UFC, he knew he had the leverage over them to negotiate, but he did not make it easy. Until UFC president Dana White agreed to sign him to a contract, Ortiz refused to step into the octagon. Many people had said he would not go back into the ring because he was afraid of fighting Chuck Liddell, a theory that seemed true, given that once Randy Couture beat Liddell, Ortiz immediately agreed to fight Couture to reaffirm his championship status. But Couture had a tough lesson waiting for Ortiz in the octagon. The veteran Couture easily handled Ortiz and literally spanked him as the fifth round came to a close. Couture won the fight by decision.

After that fight, Ortiz won a few fights and lost a few, but he never again held a championship title. The MMA world had moved beyond Ortiz and had found new stars in guys like Matt Hughes, Chuck Liddell and Georges St-Pierre. By 2006, Ortiz was making the news again; however, this time it was for his life out of the octagon, when he and porn superstar Jenna Jameson started dating. Three years later, Jameson gave birth to twins. While Ortiz is still involved in the MMA world, it is mostly from behind a desk running his "Punishment Athletics" MMA equipment and clothing company and spending time training new stars in his training center in Huntington Beach, California.

And the Winner Is...

Multidisciplinary

Fighters in the world of MMA do not rely on a single technique in fighting, hence the name mixed martial arts. Although when the UFC first began, many of the fighters were only versed in only one form of combat, such as sumo or karate, and wrestling. When they failed in competition repeatedly, fighters began to combine the various disciplines into the mixed martial arts phenomenon that exists today. Below is a list of some of the more popular styles of martial arts that are used by the best fighters.

- Brazilian jiujitsu: One of the most popular and most widely used techniques in ultimate fighting. Practitioners of this style once dominated the fighting scene, but it now provides more of a set of basic techniques for fighters to build upon.

- Karate: When the UFC first started, karate fighters were expected to do the most damage, but sadly, after a few events, karate was laughed out of the building when compared to the effectiveness of Brazilian jiujitsu. Fighters like Georges St-Pierre and Bas Rutten started out in karate, but it can barely be seen in their fights today. The only fighter to effectively use karate techniques in MMA fights has been Lyoto Machida.

- Muay thai: Considered one of the core styles in MMA fighting, muay thai uses Western boxing techniques mixed in with the old-fashioned street-fighting techniques of Thailand. A muay thai fighter uses every part of his body in a fight, but it he is most effective when standing up so he can use his fists, elbows, knees and feet to win a match.

- Boxing: Another technique used in the mixed martial artist's weaponry is boxing. Without having a basic boxing style in MMA today, no fighter would stand a chance at winning. Right hooks, upper cuts and simple avoidance defensive techniques are essential.

- Judo: Similar to jiujitsu, this Japanese martial art focuses on throws and submission techniques. A lot of current MMA fighters have a background in judo.

- Greco-Roman wrestling: When the UFC first started, and wrestler Dan Severn went into the ring against the jiujitsu of Royce Gracie, no one expected Severn to survive. Although Severn did lose the match, he proved that wrestling had the fundamental techniques necessary for success in the octagon. Shooting in for takedowns and the speed work on the ground are now essential techniques to master in MMA.

- Kickboxing: Kickboxing is a martial art combining boxing punches and martial arts kicks and is similar to muay thai in style.

Crazy War Machine

Although he was born Jon Koppenhaver, when "War Machine" joined *The Ultimate Fighter* television series in its sixth season, he thought that the nickname fit his character much better—and, well, he was right.

While his fighting skills left much to be desired, War Machine made sure he was always talked about. Besides introducing the television world to his fecal prank that he titled "The Upper

Decker" (where one defecates in the upper tank of the toilet), he made stupid claims that fighter Evan Tanner's tragic death was in fact a suicide because of the UFC neglecting its fighter. Worst of all, he posted a hate-filled, homophobic, racist tirade against President Barack Obama, going as far as claiming that he should be assassinated along with all future presidents. These tirades got the War Machine banned from the entire MMA world, but he continued to descend into insanity by getting into fights in bars, starting fights in gay bars and even trying to get into the world of pornography.

Medieval Methods

The original promoter of the UFC, Semaphore Entertainment, was already pushing the limits of entertainment by placing sumo wrestlers up against wrestlers, but what few people know is that the company wanted to take the entertainment aspect to a whole new level (maybe eight or ten levels at that). Some of the ideas were just insane. As if it wasn't enough of a spectacle to have trained fighters beating on each other bare-fisted, organizers actually wanted to include electric fencing and, believe it or not, alligator moats to surround the rings during the fights. Naturally, the UFC doctors warned against such gimmicks, and no insurance company on earth would be foolish enough to cover those kinds of dangers. So organizers brought in even bigger sumo wrestlers such as Emmanuel Yarborough.

Where's the Help?

During the first few UFC events, the referees had little power to do anything in the octagon because there were simply so few rules to enforce. Even if a fighter was being beaten to a pulp, they could not stop the fight. In the beginning, the only rules refs had to enforce were no biting, no eye gouging and no throat strikes. Eventually, after some fighter had his wits knocked out of him, referees were given the power to stop fights.

How to Settle an Argument, UFC Style

When the Fertitta brothers bought the UFC in 2001 for $2 million, they had hoped to turn around the floundering company using their business connections and ties to the Las Vegas sporting world, but just three years later, they were over $30 million in the red and on the verge of folding operations. Luckily for the brothers, they stuck with the UFC, and within another three years they had turned the struggling event into a global phenomenon that in 2006 was said to be worth over $700 million. In addition to the monetary successes of the UFC enjoyed by the Fertitta brothers, they are also passionate about the sport, going as far as including a unique clause in their ownership contract. Called a dispute resolution clause, it states that in case of a deadlock between the members of Zuffa (the name of the company owned by the Fertitta brothers that runs the UFC), the Fertitta brothers "shall engage in a sport jiujitsu match" of three five-minute rounds that are to be refereed by UFC president Dana White. To this date, the brothers have not yet entered into the octagon to resolve a contractual dispute.

Dubious Company

In order to attract the most attention, the organizers of the first UFC promoted the fights in the most violent of terms possible, describing them as being "no holds barred," "two men enter, one man leaves," and stating that the fights would only end with a "knockout, submission, or death."

The UFC did not help its cause in getting public acceptance when the first images of the fights of bloodied and toothless fighters hit the six o'clock news. This language naturally brought out a fair share of malcontents who called for an outright ban on any future events and even for the arrest of the promoters. However, one of the most overt examples of the growing hatred toward the UFC came when a public TV station, normally willing to put anything on television, refused to run an UFC advertisement. The only other organization that the station had refused air time was the Ku Klux Klan. Oh, how things have changed!

Star Power!

When the UFC was first conceived, none of the organizers really knew how to market the event because North American audiences had nothing to compare it to. The closest thing to a mixed martial arts event was boxing, so to appeal to the widest possible audience, organizers actively sought out a famous boxer to join their lineup of fighters.

Of course, Mike Tyson was the first boxer on most people's minds, but his cost was too high, given that most fighters at that time received only $1000 for one fight. The organizers settled on calling James "Bonecrusher" Smith and Leon Spinks, but neither boxer would even consider stepping into a barefisted fight. Organizers then found veteran boxer Art Jimmerson and offered him $20,000 just to show up. Of course, the Jimmerson fight was a big disappointment. After viewing the brutality of the fights, Jimmerson quit the moment Royce Gracie jumped on him and took him to the ground. You have to wonder if Leon Spinks or Mike Tyson in his prime could have put on a better show.

The King of the Web Brawlers

The world first learned of Kimbo Slice by way of his 2003 Youtube videos of him beating various challengers to a bloody pulp. His first and most popular taped fight came against a man named Big D, when Kimbo opened up a large cut above his opponent's right eye that appeared to have crushed his eyeball into a bloody smear. The gruesome nature of Kimbo's fights and his big, bald and bearded look attracted millions of viewers to Youtube and got many people wondering whether he would survive in the world of mixed martial arts. After much hype and a few more Internet videos of Kimbo beating up guys on the street, the world of MMA finally came calling. Luckily, the bearded street brawler was not all bravado, and before setting foot in the octagon, he decided to take a few lessons in martial arts from none other than Bas Rutten and a boxing instructor.

Kimbo Slice made his MMA debut fighting against former boxing WBO heavyweight champion Ray Mercer at the Cage Fury Fighting Championships 5 in Atlantic City on June 23, 2007. Although Mercer had professional boxing

Guillotine choke: The attacker places his arm around his opponent's neck, grabs his wrist with his other arm and pulls, pressing down on the trachea and the arteries in the neck.

experience, he had received only beginner lessons in mixed martial arts fighting and was easily beaten by Kimbo in just over one minute into the first round via a guillotine choke.

The fans wanted to see more of Kimbo, but many people in the ultimate fighting world did not approve of this former street brawler turned fighter, feeling that his presence brought the image of the sport back to where it was in 1996 when it was marginalized and almost legislated out of existence by people believing it to be nothing more than organized brutality. UFC heavyweight Frank Mir did not hold back his criticisms of Kimbo, saying in an interview, "Every time Kimbo Slice fights, it sets [mixed martial arts] back."

Despite the backlash against Kimbo, there was no doubt that he could still bring in fans to see him fight. After a few more fights with EliteXC promotions, Kimbo got the call everyone had been waiting for and signed on with the UFC.

But in order to gain a spot in a UFC event, Kimbo was forced to earn his place by going through UFC boot camp, better known as *The Ultimate Fighter* TV series. His appearance on the show, however, turned out to be a complete failure. In the first fight of the show, he was defeated in the second round by Roy Nelson via TKO when the ref stopped the fight because of repeated punches to Kimbo's head. This was the first time Kimbo had been placed in an arena with a quality opponent, and he lost in an embarrassing fashion. Many of his fans finally began to question whether the seemingly unbeatable street fighter could live up to his own hype.

Dana White gave Kimbo one more chance with an official heavyweight fight at UFC 113 in May 2010 against Matt Mitrione. At the outset of the fight, it was obvious to everyone in attendance that Kimbo had lost much of his mystique when placed in the octagon with trained fighters. He managed to hold his own in some fights, but up against guys like Mitrione, Kimbo looked like an amateur. After losing the fight to Mitrione in the second round, Kimbo has not since made it back into the octagon.

Common Myths about Mixed Martial Arts

For anyone showing interest in MMA training, there is bound to be someone who has brought up at least one of the following common misconceptions about the sport, ranging from the curious to the ridiculous.

Myth: MMA is a very dangerous sport, and fighters endanger their lives every time they step in the ring.

Fact: Ultimate fighters have rigorous training schedules that would put other athletes to shame. Making sure their bodies are in peak physical conditioning before a fight is what helps to prevent injury. Before a fight, every MMA athlete is given a complete physical, and several doctors stand ready at ringside should any serious injury occur during a bout. Ambulance attendants are also on standby, and after the match is over, all fighters must once again get checked by a doctor. On top of that, each fighter is subject to strict drug testing to maintain fair play and to ensure that the athletes do not do harm to themselves. In the history of MMA fighting, only a handful of deaths have been related to a fight. Boxing on average has 10 to 15 deaths per year attributed to injuries suffered from repeated blows to the head.

Myth: Mixed martial arts is a fringe sport that only appeals to young men looking for violent entertainment.

Fact: It is true that when mixed martial arts was first introduced to the world, most devotees of the sport were young males from the ages of 15 to 30, but in the last five years, the sport has found appeal among all age groups and genders. It took a lot of work, but now, sponsors from Viacom to Gatorade have come calling after recognizing the potential market. With UFC events selling out 55,000-seat stadiums, mixed martial arts is no longer something your little brother practiced in the basement with his friends. The sport is global and attracts more fans every year.

Myth: Mixed martial arts is the same as no-rules street fighting.

Fact: Even when the UFC first started and it was advertised as no-rules fighting, there were still a few rules in place to ensure the safety of the fighters, such as no eye gouging and no biting. Back then, state athletic commissions wouldn't support the events, and lawmakers even wondered whether it was illegal to have grown men fighting each other in such a manner. To achieve a certain status and acceptance, the MMA community was forced to adapt and change its ways by adopting a more strict set of guidelines. Today, all sanctioned MMA events are governed under the *Unified Rules of Mixed Martial Arts,* which details how the sport is to function, just as boxing, baseball and hockey have their own set of guidelines. In addition, there are weight classes and time limits on rounds. A total of 31 individual rules ensure the sport is taken seriously by all participants.

Myth: Mixed martial arts was once banned in every U.S. state.

Fact: Only the state of New York enacted a specific ban on mixed martial arts fighting. In fact, even with the rise in popularity of the UFC and other organizations, and an increasing public acceptance of MMA, the statute remains in New York law books to this day. No other state ever passed a law banning the fights—even the great state of Arizona, where ultimate fighting's most vocal opponent, John McCain, just happened to be senator, didn't ban the sport.

Myth: MMA is debasing our culture and contributing to the increase of violence in society.

Fact: Although the fights appear to be bloody and violent to the uninitiated, those who practice the disciplines of judo, Greco-Roman wrestling, jiujitsu and so on are taught respect for others, and in real life, they are some of the most relaxed people in the world. The true fans of MMA are well aware of this. Because of the effectiveness of the fighting style, many women's self-defense classes are springing up across the globe that teach techniques that come straight out of the octagon.

Fast Facts

- Mixed martial arts has attained a new level of popularity. The UFC has its own line of video games, and Georges St-Pierre is advertising for Gatorade.

- The annual percentage growth of pay-per-view buys of ultimate fighting has increased from 47 percent in 2004 (over 2003) to 189 percent in 2005 and 352 percent in 2006.

- Gross revenues of pay-per-view MMA events has had annual increases of 47 percent in 2004, 232 percent in 2005, and 424 percent in 2006.

- A total of 55 hours per month of television programming in the U.S. focus on MMA, on channels including Fox, FSN, Spike TV, National Geographic Channel, Discovery Channel and in syndication.

- Mixed martial arts has had an average growth rate over the past four years of almost 390 percent, in terms of hours of monthly television programming featuring MMA.

- One of the first American mixed martial artists was President Theodore Roosevelt, who held a brown belt in judo and who wrestled and boxed in his younger years.

- Randy Couture, Mark Coleman, Chuck Liddell, Royce Gracie, Matt Hughes, Charles Lewis, Dan Severn and Ken Shamrock all belong to the UFC Hall of Fame.

- Dan Severn had no professional fighting record to speak of when he entered the UFC, and he filled out an application in a magazine to apply. There was no "Wrestling" category, so he checked "Other." The UFC was wary of this, not wanting to sign an unskilled fighter, and in order to be cleared, Severn had to sign a contract stating, "In case of your accidental death, we are not liable."

- UFC 129, held in Toronto, Canada, in April 2011, was the first UFC event held in a stadium. The Rogers Centre, normally the home of the Toronto Blue Jays, played host to the 55,000 spectators who gathered to watch Canadian champion Georges St-Pierre defend his title against American Jake Shields. St-Pierre won.

- Rorion Gracie, one of the original creators of the UFC, had previously worked as a fight coordinator for the Hollywood blockbuster *Lethal Weapon*, starring Mel Gibson and Danny Glover.

- Dan Severn wrote several articles on mixed martial arts for *Penthouse* magazine.

- Matt Serra was the first American to whom the Gracie Academy awarded a black belt.

- Before entering into the UFC, Gary Goodridge was a world champion arm-wrestler and had only two courses on submission techniques. His inexperience in his first fight did not matter when he knocked out his opponent with a series of vicious elbows to the head.

- Chuck Liddell played a boy scout in the 1981 film *The Postman Always Rings Twice*, starring Jack Nicholson and Jessica Lange.

- Tank Abbott has a degree in history, and Chuck Liddell has a Bachelor of Arts in accounting.

- Frank Shamrock (Ken Shamrock's adopted brother) was born Frank Alisio Juarez III.

- Russian tough guy Fedor Emelianenko has a pet turtle.

- MMA fighter Aaron Brink started out his career in show business as a porn star before moving over to cage fighting.

- When Ukrainian fighter Igor Vovchanchyn was a child growing up in the small village of Zolochiv, he was known to have an explosive temper. Whenever he would get angry, the villagers would ring a bell, and everyone would hide in their homes until he calmed down.

- Before getting the nickname "Cro Cop," fighter Mirco Filipovic's nickname was "Tiger."

- Quinton "Rampage" Jackson made the leap from the octagon to the Hollywood stage when he played the iconic 1980s television character B.A. Baracus in the 2010 movie *The A-Team*. Baracus was, of course, originally played by the legendary Mr. T. But Rampage Jackson's acting resumé does not begin there. In 2006, he played a delivery truck driver in the TV series *The King of Queens*, and in 2008 he played a New York subway security officer known as a Guardian Angel in Clive Barker's horror film *The Midnight Meat Train*.

- Another unusual fact about Rampage Jackson is that although he has one of the meanest-looking faces on earth that no one would ever dare mess with (except Chuck Norris, of course), Jackson is deathly allergic to bees.

- In 2001, when Rampage Jackson traveled to Japan to fight in Pride, the Japanese, who liked to associate the fighters with a certain type of character, marketed him as being a homeless person.

- Although Georges St-Pierre can now buy any vehicle he wants, his first car was a Ford Tempo.

- In the MMA, Joe Son is best known as the fighter in UFC 4 who was repeatedly punched in the groin by Keith Hackney (at the time, the UFC had no rules against groin strikes, but up until that fight, no other fighter had dared cross that sacred line). Outside of the MMA world, Son is better known as Random Task from the 1997 movie *Austin Powers: International Man of Mystery*. The Random Task character was a parody of the character Oddjob from the James Bond movie *Goldfinger*. Although Oddjob killed his enemies by throwing a bladed hat at their heads, Random Task tried to kill his enemies with a shoe. (Seriously, who throws a shoe?)

- Randy Couture holds the current record for most title fights in his career, with 14. His record in those bouts is nine wins and five losses.

- Before Matt Serra handed Georges St-Pierre one of his only two career losses, he began his martial arts training as a young man by studying kung fu in his home town of East Meadow, New York.

- MMA fighter Drew Fickett is in a band called…wait for it…Cock Sandwich.

- Zuffa, parent company of the UFC, is Italian slang for "scuffle."

- UFC ring announcer Bruce Buffer holds a black belt in jiujitsu and once fought as a kickboxer.

- UFC president Dana White was once a hotel bellboy.

- In the early days of the UFC, Dana White used to manage Chuck Liddell and Tito Ortiz.

- UFC owners Frank and Lorenzo Fertitta both made the 2011 Forbes billionaire list at 1057th and 1140th place, respectively.

- In 2006, for the first time in prizefighting televised history, a UFC event sold five million pay-per-view subscriptions, beating out perennial champions boxing and wrestling.

Fantastic Quotes from the MMA World

I will beat you into a living death.

–Ken Shamrock, to one of his unlucky opponents
(Note: although I could not find who Shamrock
was speaking to, I assume from their history of
hatred that he was speaking to Tito Ortiz.)

It's an octagonal octagon.

–Bill Wallace, announcer at UFC 1

I don't know what kind of technique was used there, but there was a lot of kicking and punching.

–Jim Brown

I dreamed that I was being raped by Freddy Mercury.

–Tank Abbott, after losing to Dan Severn, who was said to resemble the lead singer of the rock band Queen

Mike Tyson's a great boxer. The greatest boxer—but boxer. Not the best fighter.

–Royce Gracie

A black belt only covers two inches of your ass. You have to cover the rest.

–Royce Gracie

You put the Devil on the other side, and I will come to fight.

–Royce Gracie

The idea of jiujitsu is to give the little guy a chance to beat the big guy.

–Royce Gracie

When we first bought the company, the only thing we ended up buying was the name.... This guy had stripped it down and sold everything away. The company was in a lot of trouble. Basically, they were on their last show.

–Dana White, speaking of when Zuffa purchased the UFC from Semaphore

It was around 1997 or 1998 that it all turned around for us. We were all boxing guys and I used to think UFC was a joke. I would say, "Those guys would get their asses kicked by a boxer."

–Dana White

What's more violent than boxing? You and I stand in front of each other for 12 rounds, and my goal is to hit you so hard in the face that I knock you unconscious. In the UFC, you and I can fight, and I can beat you and win, and never punch you in the head once. We can go right to the ground, start grappling, and pull off a submission. It's not 25, 30 minutes of blows to the head non-stop.

–Dana White

When we first bought the company, there was the stigma attached to the UFC.... At that time, we were out trying to talk to venues. Venues weren't even interested in having the UFC there. MGM, Mandalay Bay, a few out in Atlantic City. We had to go in and get people interested in hosting UFC events.

–Dana White

That's one of the things when you go to a UFC event live, the energy in the place is crazy. People are there because they're passionate about it.

–Dana White

Boxing is a road map of what not to do. The greedy promoters basically killed the sport by taking it off free TV.

–Dana White

If you take four street corners, and on one they are playing baseball, on another they are playing basketball and on the other, street hockey. On the fourth corner, a fight breaks out. Where does the crowd go? They all go to the fight.

–Dana White

You want to know why he's the greatest fighter on the planet today? That is why! Tim Sylvia is shaking his head in disbelief! That, folks, is the Michael Jordan, the Tiger Woods, the Rocky Marciano of our sport!

–Senior Fox Sports writer Jay Glazer on Fedor Emelianenko

When I started, I used to go off just instincts. Then they took head butts away, so I had to learn some skills.

–Mark Coleman

After a match, my opponent goes to the hospital and gets an IV, and I have a martini.

–Tank Abbott

I like Tito. I like a lot of people, but I'll fight every one of 'em. It's all business. When I step into the octagon, it's all business.

–Chuck Liddell on fighting Tito Ortiz

I've never been hit flush in the face before.

–Emmanuel Yarborough after his first fight in the UFC octagon

If size mattered, the elephant would be the king of the jungle.

–Anderson Silva

I will knock your hair black.

–Ken Shamrock to a blond Tito Ortiz

I only want to be known as the best ever. Is that too much to ask?

–B.J. Penn

I knew I 'urt 'im when he said "aarg."

–Georges St-Pierre

Well, I'm 22 right now, so in three years I see myself being 25.

–Rampage Jackson when he was asked where he saw himself
in three years

The best way for jiujitsu athletes to win isn't by confronting an opponent in the other person's strongest art. Yes, you have to understand the other arts so you can solve them. And the solution is jiujitsu. Neutralize their game and bring the match to your area of expertise. This is where you have a much better chance to win.

–Rickson Gracie

I know what the fans like, I know what the fans want to see. I give them a show. I lose sometimes, because I take chances. But I have more respect from my fans and the fighters. My fans know I give everything I have. Win or lose, that's just one part of the fight. A good show. I want to give fans a good show. This is entertainment, not just a fight.

–Wanderlei Silva on fighting

There is no comparison though between a street fight and where I am right now as a professional fighter. A street fight is one-dimensional. All you have to worry about is a guy throwing punches. You don't have to worry about nothing except getting knocked the f*** out. In mixed martial arts, you have to train and be prepared. These guys have skills and these guys are professionals. And you can be hurt.

–Kimbo Slice

Philosophy helped me with my fighting. I can show you many examples. It's like war. We've seen it in the past: the country or civilization with the most advanced weapons wins the war.... I want to have a weapon that nobody else has. That's why I've been traveling a lot. I want to have some techniques, some weapons, so I can win and dominate my sport. That's what I need to have to stay ahead of the game.

–Georges St-Pierre

...it's like a chest match.

–Tito Ortiz (using the wrong vocabulary in talking strategy, on *The Ultimate Fighter*)

Notes on Sources

Print Sources

Ehrenreich, Barbara. *Blood Rites*. New York: Henry Holt and Company, 1997.

Gracie, Renzo, and John Danaher. *Mastering JujItsu*. Windsor: Human Kinetics, 2003.

Gracie, Rodrigo, and Kid Peligro. *No Holds Barred*. Invisible Cities Press: Montpellier, 2005.

Krauss, Erich. *UFC: As Real as it Gets*. New York: Citadel Press, 2004.

Penn, B.J., and Glen Cordoza, et al, *Mixed Martial Arts: The Book of Knowledge*. Los Angeles: Victory Belt Publishing, 2007.

Sheridan, Sam. *The Fighter's Mind*. New York: Grove Press, 2010.

——. *A Fighter's Heart*. New York: Grove Press, 2007.

Snowden, Jonathan. *Total MMA: Inside Ultimate Fighting*. Toronto: ECW Press, 2008.

Snowden, Jonathan, and Kendall Shields. *The MMA Encyclopedia*. Toronto: ECW Press, 2010.

Web Sources

http://ejmas.com/jcs/jcsart_svinth_a_0700.htm

http://mmaweekly.com/

http://stickgrappler.tripod.com/bjj/bad.html

www.aikidojournal.com/article.php?articleID=17

www.associatedcontent.com/article/83188/is_ultimate_
fighting_safer_than_boxing.html

www.bstkd.com/JudoHistory/HistoryTwo.htm

www.kenshamrock.com/biography/

www.mmafighting.com/

www.mmatorch.com/artman2/publish/DVD_
Reviews_17/article_161.shtml

www.sherdog.com/

www.strikeforce.com/

www.ufc.com/

J. Alexander Poulton

J. Alexander Poulton is a writer, photographer and genuine Canadian sports enthusiast. A resident of Montreal all his life, he has been know to "call in sick" during the broadcasts of major sports events so that he can get in as much viewing in as possible.

He earned his BA in English literature from McGill University and his graduate diploma in journalism from Concordia University. He has 25 other sports books to his credit, including books on hockey, baseball, soccer, curling and the Olympics. However, the martial arts have been a part of his personal life for many years.